ore Rosa Parks, there was Claudette Colvin, a teenager who
 her constitutional rights and was willing to get arrested to
 it . . . Hoose gives new immediacy to one of the civil rights
ement's monumental achievements: the Montgomery bus
ott."   —*The Washington Post*

llip Hoose gives depth and context to the larger-than-life,
etimes mythologized history of the civil rights movement . . .
ay Colvin . . . has been virtually forgotten. Hoose's book,
d in part on interviews with Colvin and people who knew her,
ly gives her the credit she deserves."
                        —*The New York Times Book Review*

ose makes the moments in Montgomery come alive, whether
about Claudette's neighborhood, her attorneys, her pastor or
he different individuals in the civil rights movement whose
 s she crossed . . . An engrossing read."   —*Chicago Tribune*

day, thanks to Hoose, a new generation of girls—and boys—
 add Claudette Colvin to their list of heroines."
                        —*The Christian Science Monitor*

mpelling."   —*New York Daily News*

ose vividly recreates Colvin's bravery."   —*New York Post*

illip Hoose weaves together the richly detailed memories of
 now-septuagenarian Colvin into the context of the burgeoning
l rights movement and the brutal oppression of Jim Crow
 th that treated black Americans as second-class citizens."
                                                  —Oprah.com

Winner of the National Book Av

A Newbery Honor Book

A Robert F. Sibert Honor Bo

A YALSA Finalist for Excellence in N

An ALA Best Book for Young A

An ALA Notable Children's B

A *Washington Post* Best Kid's Book

A *Publishers Weekly* Best Children's Bo

Fanfare, *The Horn Book*'s Hono

A *Booklist* Editors' Choice

A *School Library Journal* Best Book

A *Kirkus Reviews* Best Young Adu

An Amazon.com Top 10 Book:

A Jane Addams Children's Book Award

A New York Public Library Top 100 Book for

A Chicago Public Library Best of the Best Re

★ "This inspiring title shows the incredible difference that a single young person can make, even as it demonstrates the multitude of interconnected lives that create and sustain a political movement." —STARRED / *Booklist*

★ "Well-written and engaging . . . Outstanding." —STARRED / *School Library Journal*

★ "Hoose's evenhanded account investigates Colvin's motives and influences, and carefully establishes the historical context so that readers can appreciate both Colvin's maturity and bravery and the boycott leadership's pragmatism." —STARRED / *Publishers Weekly*

★ "Hoose reasserts [Claudette Colvin's] place in history with this vivid and dramatic account, complemented with photographs, sidebars, and liberal excerpts from interviews conducted with Colvin . . . Thoughtful." —STARRED / *The Horn Book*

"Offers a glimpse at a long-overlooked figure in the civil rights movement, who is now credited with being an important factor in sparking the Montgomery bus boycott . . . [A] fresh look at a well-documented period in American history." —*VOYA*

"Not only does Hoose's account, liberally laced with quotes from interviews he conducted with Colvin, set the record straight, it is an inspiration to all young people about the sweeping changes that can come from one brave act and a belief in doing the right thing." —*Shelf Awareness*

ALSO BY PHILLIP HOOSE

Building an Ark: Tools for the Preservation of Natural Diversity Through Land Protection

Hoosiers: The Fabulous Basketball Life of Indiana

Necessities: Racial Barriers in American Sports

It's Our World, Too!: Young People Who Are Making a Difference

Hey, Little Ant (with Hannah Hoose)

We Were There, Too!: Young People in U.S. History

The Race to Save the Lord God Bird

Perfect, Once Removed: When Baseball Was All the World to Me

Moonbird: A Year on the Wind with the Great Survivor B95

CLAUDETTE COLVIN

COLVIN

TWICE TOWARD JUSTICE

BY PHILLIP HOOSE

FARRAR STRAUS GIROUX
NEW YORK

FARRAR
STRAUS
GIROUX

SQUARE
FISH

Imprints of Macmillan
175 Fifth Avenue
New York, New York 10010
mackids.com

Square Fish and the Square Fish logo are trademarks of Macmillan
and are used by Farrar Straus Giroux under license from Macmillan.

Originally published in the United States by Melanie Kroupa Books,
an imprint of Farrar Straus Giroux
Square Fish logo designed by Filomena Tuosto
First Square Fish Edition: December 2011

ISBN 978-0-374-30236-8 (FSG hardcover)
1   3   5   7   9   10   8   6   4   2

ISBN 978-0-312-66105-2 (Square Fish paperback)
9   11   13   12   10   8

AR: 6.8 / LEXILE: 1000L

Library of Congress Cataloging-in-Publication Data
Hoose, Phillip M., date.
   Claudette Colvin : twice toward justice / by Phillip Hoose.— 1st ed.
      p. cm.
   Includes bibliographical references and index.
   ISBN 978-0-312-66105-2
   1. Colvin, Claudette, 1939- —Juvenile literature.   2. African Americans—Alabama—
Montgomery—Biography—Juvenile literature.   3. African American civil rights workers—
Alabama—Montgomery—Biography—Juvenile literature.   4. African American teenage
girls—Alabama—Montgomery—Biography—Juvenile literature.   5. African Americans—
Segregation—Alabama—Montgomery—History—Juvenile literature.   6. Segregation in
transportation—Alabama—Montgomery—History—Juvenile literature   7. Montgomery
(Ala.)—Biography—Juvenile literature.   8. Montgomery (Ala.)—Race relations—History—
20th century—Juvenile literature.   I. Title.

F334.M753C6554 2009
323.092—dc22
   [B]
                                                                    2008005435

"The Black Man Speaks," from *The Collected Poems of Langston Hughes* by Langston Hughes,
edited by Arnold Rampersad with David Roessel, associate editor, copyright © 1994 by the Estate
of Langston Hughes. Used by permission of Alfred A. Knopf, a division of Random House, Inc.

"Still I Rise," copyright © 1978 by Maya Angelou, from *And Still I Rise* by Maya Angelou. Used
by permission of Random House, Inc.

To Gerald E. Talbot,
for keeping alive the history of African-American life in Maine
—P.H.

CONTENTS

PART ONE

FIRST CRY

Injustice anywhere is a threat to justice everywhere.
—Dr. Martin Luther King, Jr.

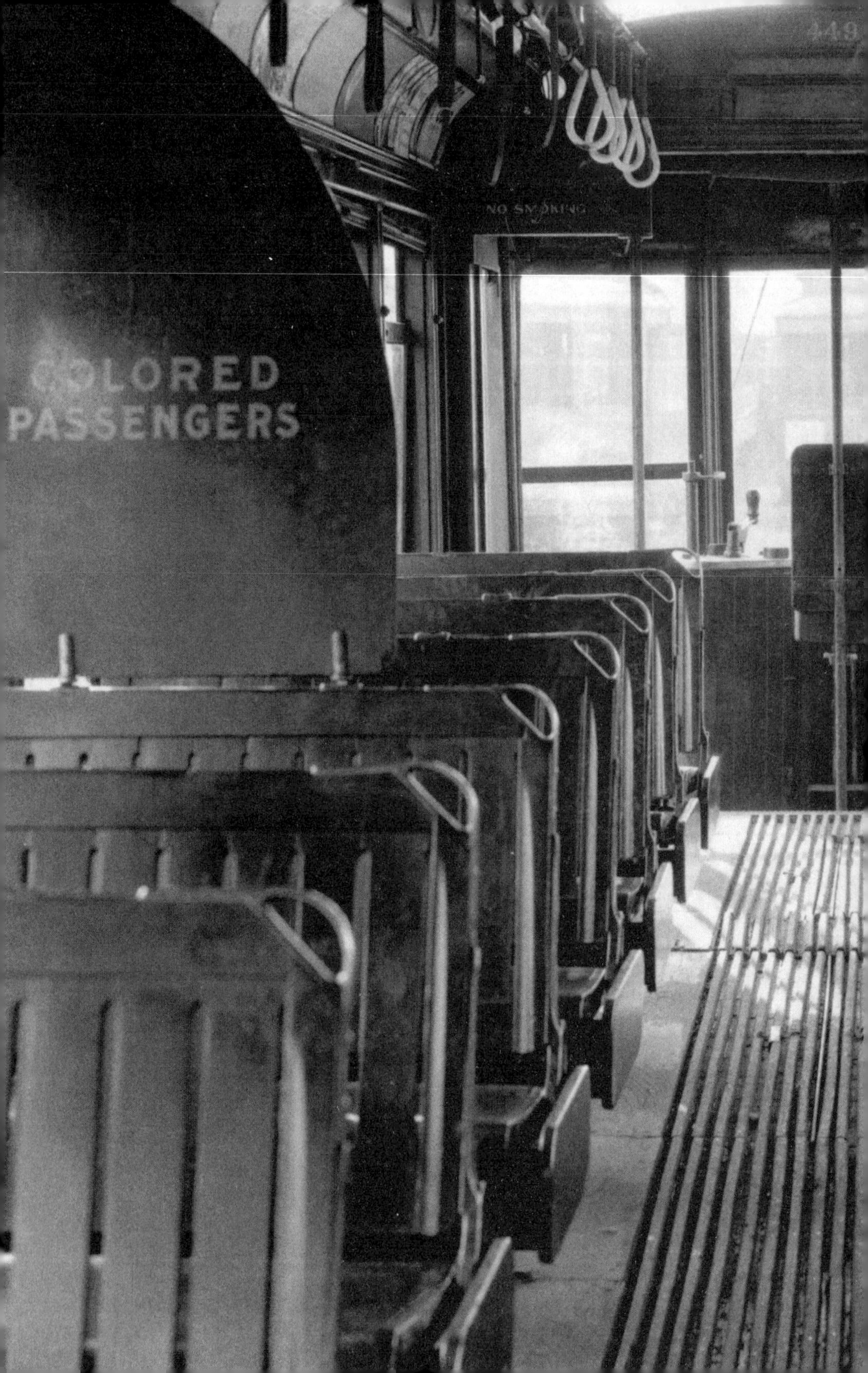
COLORED
PASSENGERS
NO SMOKING

CHAPTER ONE

JIM CROW AND THE DETESTED NUMBER TEN

I swear to the Lord
I still can't see
Why Democracy means
Everybody but me.
    —Langston Hughes

CLAUDETTE COLVIN: I was about four years old the first time I ever saw what happened when you acted up to whites. I was standing in line at the general store when this little white boy cut in front of me. Then some older white kids came in through the door and started laughing. I turned around to see what they were laughing at. They were pointing at me. The little white boy said, "Let me see, let me see, too." For some reason they all wanted to see my hands. I held my hands up, palms out, and he put his hands up against my hands. Touched them. The older kids doubled up laughing. My mother saw us, and she saw that the boy's mother was watching. Then my mom came straight across the room, raised her hand, and gave me a backhand slap across my face. I burst into tears. She said, "Don't you know you're not supposed to touch them?" The white boy's mother nodded at my mom and said, "That's right, Mary."

That's how I learned I should never touch another white person again.

• • •

IF, LIKE CLAUDETTE COLVIN, you grew up black in central Alabama during the 1940s and 1950s, Jim Crow controlled your life from womb to tomb. Black and white babies were born in separate hospitals, lived their adult lives apart from one another, and were buried in separate cemeteries. The races were segregated by a dense, carefully woven web of laws, signs, partitions, arrows, ordinances, unequal opportunities, rules, insults, threats, and customs—often backed up by violence. Together, the whole system of racial segregation was known as "Jim Crow."

Jim Crow's job was not only to separate the races but to keep blacks poor. In 1950, nearly three in five black women in Montgomery, Alabama's capital city, worked as maids for white families, and almost three-quarters of employed black men mowed lawns and did other kinds of unskilled labor. The average black worker made about half as much money as the average white. "The only professional jobs . . . open to blacks were . . . pastoring a black church and schoolteaching, which was open because of segregated schools," recalled the Reverend Ralph Abernathy, the minister of the First Baptist Church in Montgomery during the 1950s.

Jim Crow kept blacks and whites from learning together, playing or eating meals together, working or riding buses or trains together, worshiping with one another, even going up and down in the same elevator or throwing a ball back and forth in the same park. Black and white citizens drank water from separate fountains and used different bathrooms. They were forbidden to play sports on the same team, marry one another, or swim together in the same pool.

Some of the segregation laws didn't matter too much in the daily lives of black citizens, but the bus was different. Riding the bus was like having a sore tooth that never quit aching. Montgomery's neighborhoods were spread out, and the maids and "yard boys"—people like Claudette Colvin's parents who scraped together a few dollars a day by attending to the needs of

WHO WAS JIM CROW?

Between the 1830s and the 1950s, minstrel shows starred white performers who smeared burnt cork on their faces and ridiculed African-American life. Thomas "Daddy" Rice is credited with popularizing minstrel shows with the song "Jump Jim Crow," which, he said, he'd heard from a black singer. After the sheet music sold widely, Jim Crow became a standard character in minstrel shows and then evolved into a term to represent the whole system of laws and customs that segregated black and white Americans.

white families—depended on the buses to reach the homes of their white employers. Thousands of students also rode the buses to school from the time they were little, learning the transfer points and schedules by heart. They gathered in clusters at the corners, chatting and teasing and cramming for tests, until the green and gold buses chugged into view and the doors snapped open. Most blacks *had* to ride the bus.

But everything about riding a bus was humiliating for black passengers. All riders entered through the front door and dropped their dimes in the fare box near the driver. But, unless the entire white section was empty, blacks alone had to get back off the bus and reenter through the rear door. Sometimes the driver pulled away while black passengers were still standing outside.

In other Southern cities, like Atlanta and Nashville and Mobile, black passengers sat in the back and whites sat in the front of the bus, with the two groups coming together in the middle as the bus filled up. When all the seats were taken, riders of both races stood.

But Montgomery had its own rules and traditions. Here, each bus had thirty-six seats. The first four rows of seats, which held ten passengers, were reserved for white passengers only. Day after day weary black passengers remained standing over empty seats in front. Trying to hold on to their packages and small children, they jostled for balance even as the aisles became jammed with dozens of seatless passengers. Seating behind the first ten seats was up to the driver, who constantly glanced into the mirror above his head to keep track of who was sitting where. If the ten white

The Jim Crow South

seats in front were filled, the driver ordered black passengers to surrender their seats in the middle and rear of the bus to newly boarding white passengers. In fact, if even one white passenger wanted to sit in a row occupied by four black riders, the driver would glance up and yell, "I need those seats!" All four blacks were expected to stand up and make their way to the rear.

It didn't matter if they were elderly, pregnant, ill, or balancing children on their laps. It also didn't matter that the city bus law—or ordinance, as city laws are called—had said since 1900 that no rider had to give up a seat unless another was available. Drivers simply ignored the law until it became customary for blacks to move when the driver told them to. When he said to get up, he expected people to get up, and they did. If there were no seats left in the rear, black passengers were simply out of luck.

The Montgomery City Lines bus company hired tough men to command their buses. And Montgomery's city ordinance gave them police powers. Every driver understood from the day he was hired that his main job, other than driving the bus, was to enforce the Jim Crow rules. Some drivers carried pistols.

Having to stand up at the end of a long day within plain sight of an empty seat was both depressing and infuriating. "The ten empty seats became an obsession to weary workers," wrote Jo Ann Robinson, an English professor at Alabama State College at the time.

In 1886, Montgomery became the first city in the Western Hemisphere to convert a street railway system to electricity. The trolley line was proudly known as the Lightning Route. Twenty years later, on November 23, 1906, Montgomery also became the first U.S. city to totally segregate public transportation. A city ordinance passed on that day said blacks in all public accommodations had to be completely separated from whites. Despite the grumblings of the trolley company owners, who did not want to pay for new cars, totally separate trolley cars for blacks were established.

"The number *ten* became a damnable number . . . Nobody wanted that number on anything that belonged to him." And being packed together inside a small tube magnified the rudeness of segregation. "There were no Negro drivers," recalled Martin Luther King, Jr., of the Montgomery buses. "It was not uncommon to hear [drivers] referring to Negro passengers as . . . 'black cows' and 'black apes.'"

Over the years, a few black riders stood up to the drivers. In 1946 Geneva Johnson was arrested for "talking back" to a driver and not having the correct change. Charged with disorderly conduct, she paid a fine and her case was dismissed. A few years later Viola White and Katie Wingfield were arrested for sitting in seats reserved for whites. They also pleaded guilty and paid fines.

In the summer of 1949, sixteen-year-old Edwina Johnson and her brother Marshall, one year younger, had come down from New Jersey to visit relatives in Montgomery. During their stay they climbed aboard a city bus and sat down next to a white man and his son. The white boy ordered Marshall to move. Deeply offended, Marshall refused. The driver twice ordered the Johnsons to the back, but they stayed put. Why should things be different here than back home? The exasperated driver radioed police, who were waiting at the next stop to arrest them. When Edwina and Marshall's relatives were called, they hurried to the police station, paid the teenagers' fines, and got them out of jail. Soon the Johnsons, shaken, were on their way back to New Jersey.

It could get rougher. A driver showered insults upon a woman named

Epsie Worthy when she refused to pay an extra fare at a transfer point. Ms. Worthy got off the bus rather than pay more, only to have the driver follow her outside and begin punching her. She fought back with her fists, exchanging a flurry of blows with the driver, who spat upon her as he struck her. Police separated the two and charged Ms. Worthy with disorderly conduct.

The most shocking incident of all happened in 1952, when a man named Hilliard Brooks boarded a City Lines bus, dropped a dime in the fare box, and headed down the aisle toward the back. The driver shouted at Brooks to come back, get off, and reboard through the rear door. Brooks said he'd rather walk and asked for his dime back. The driver refused, an argument heated up, and the driver called police. An officer soon boarded the bus, ordering Brooks off. Brooks wouldn't budge until he got his dime back. The policeman shot him, and Brooks later died of his wounds. The coroner ruled his death justifiable homicide, justifiable because the officer said Brooks had been resisting arrest.

The few passengers who defied the drivers usually cooled off at the police station, paid their fines, and tried to put their humiliating experiences behind them. Why fight? The white judges, the intimidating police, the insulting drivers, and the crushing weight of all the years of custom and law were simply overwhelming.

But change was in the wind. On Monday, May 17, 1954, in the case of *Brown v. Board of Education of Topeka*, the U.S. Supreme Court outlawed racial segregation in public schools. It was a solid punch to Jim Crow, one that produced powerful shock waves throughout the South. The ruling allowed black students to anticipate a different future and emboldened a few of them to try to make it happen.

One such student was fifteen-year-old Claudette Colvin, whose school had been studying black history almost nonstop for a solid month. Around 3:30 on March 2, 1955, this slim, bespectacled high school junior boarded the Highland Gardens bus with a few of her friends and slid into a window seat on the left side, behind the white section. She piled her textbooks on her lap, smoothed her blue dress, and settled back for a five-block ride that not only would change the course of her life but would spark the most important social movement in U.S. history.

Members of Claudette's family about 1950:
(back row) Claudette's birth mother, Mary Jane Gadson, and her
husband, Thomas Gadson; (front row from left) Claudette's sisters
Delphine, Jo Ann, and Mary Ellen, and, at far right, Claudette

CHAPTER TWO

COOT

To me, God loved everyone. Why would He curse just us?
—Claudette Colvin

CLAUDETTE: I was born Claudette Austin, September 5, 1939, in Birmingham. My mom named me after Claudette Colbert, a movie star back then, supposedly because we both had high cheekbones. My biological father's name is C. P. Austin, and my birth mother's name is Mary Jane Gadson. C.P. left my mother to look for a job, stayed away for a year, and came back just long enough for my sister Delphine to be born. Then he took off again. When he came back a third time and wanted to stay, my mother finally said no.

When I was just a baby I went off to live with my great-aunt, Mary Ann Colvin, and my great-uncle, Q. P. Colvin, in a little country town called Pine Level, about thirty miles down Highway 231 from Montgomery.

Mary Ann and Q.P. are the ones I call Mom and Dad. They were a lot older than my birth parents, more like my grandparents' age, but I loved them both, and I was happy to be with them. I think the reason they took me is that their only child, Velma, was away teaching school most of the year, so they had plenty of room for me. Later Delphine came to live with us, too. So I grew up in a quartet—Mary Ann, Q.P., Delphine, and me. And our dog, Bell, and two horses and lots of chickens, cows, and pigs.

Back then, while World War II was going on, whenever one of our hens would lay a bad egg we'd mark it with an "H"—for Hitler.

People always said I was smart. I don't know about that, but I was inquisitive for sure. I wondered about everything and asked about everything: Why don't the stars fall? Where is Japan? Is it different from China? How did God make the earth so fast, in six days? Did He make the stars, too? When Bell died would she go to heaven? Shouldn't Easter be on a Monday? Weren't there supposed to be three days after the Crucifixion— so it'd be Saturday, Sunday, Monday, right?

The biggest mystery of all was how the white man came to dominate us. In the South, it was taught that white people were better than blacks. Somehow, they were the masters and we were there to work for them. My mom said white people thought God made them special. My Sunday school teacher said we had been cursed by one of Noah's sons. I didn't buy that at all. To me, God loved everyone. Why would He curse just us? My mom thought she was as good as anyone else. So did I. One day I told my pastor, Reverend H. H. Johnson, "I don't want to serve a God that would have a cursed race." He seemed proud of me for saying that.

I was a tomboy, tall and skinny and very fast, and I loved to be outdoors. I could climb trees as well as anyone. My best friend, Annie Ruth Baines, and I knew every trail and shortcut from Pine Level to our homes. A No Trespassing sign meant nothing at all to us. In the summer we would count the insect tracks in the sand across the road and try to figure out what bug made which track. We were walking to school together the first time we ever got close to a skunk, right out in the middle of the road. We ran up to pet it and got sprayed. The teacher took one sniff and sent us home.

Pine Level didn't have much more than a few shacks for the sharecropper families, a schoolhouse, a church, and a general store, but I was at home in all of it. I floated free, and slept at the homes of my mom's friends as much as in my own bed. They all raised me together. Some nights I ended up at Baby Tell's house—she was my mom's best friend, plump and short and always happy to see me. She lived in an old farmhouse, the biggest house in Pine Level. White people used to own it, and we never knew exactly how Baby Tell's family got it. Her attic was full of paintings and an organ and an old spinning wheel. Annie and I used to look out the attic window and pretend the Yankee soldiers were about ready to come charging over the hill.

Other nights I slept at Mama Sweetie's, a tiny woman in her sixties who was the best reader in Pine Level. She had read the entire Bible many times. She had her own blue-covered Webster's dictionary. Mama Sweetie taught practically every child in Pine Level their ABCs and how to write their names and how to count to a hundred, using peanuts. She cooked for all the people when they came in from the fields. Baby Tell and Mama Sweetie were like sisters to my mom, and mothers to me. They loved me to keep them company. My nonstop talking and constant questions seemed to drive my mom crazy, but it didn't bother them at all: they loved that about me.

Our school was a one-room white wooden building with red trim. Annie and I walked there together every day, lunch sacks in one hand, book sacks in the other. It had a potbellied stove in the middle and a

Spring Hill School in Pine Level, where Claudette attended elementary school, was newer than the school in rural Georgia pictured here, but like many schools for African-American children, it had one room, one teacher, six grades, and a potbellied stove for heat

picture of Abraham Lincoln on the wall. One teacher taught all six elementary grades, and sat us in sections around the room, grade by grade, two to a desk. The room was rarely full because students kept getting pulled away to do farmwork. A farmer would just appear in the doorway and yell, "I need two boys to help with the cows," and they'd be out the door in a flash.

I loved school. I memorized the Dick and Jane reader so my teacher would think I could already read. One day she asked me to read aloud, but I got way out ahead of the text. She couldn't figure out what was going on. She told my parents to take me to Montgomery to get my eyes checked. I learned the entire second grade in advance just by listening to Annie—she was a year older than me—and by hearing Mama Sweetie read from her Bible and her Webster's dictionary. When it came time for me to start second grade I could already read and write and spell and even do some arithmetic. They tested me and told me to go sit with the third graders. After that, I was always younger than the other kids in my class.

I knew plenty of white people, and they knew me. You had to be very careful around them. They never called the adults "Mr." or "Miss" or "Mrs."; they used their first names instead. Or sometimes they made up little nicknames to dominate us. I was Coot. A doctor gave that name to me when I was little to distract me from the shot he was about to give. He sang, "Oh she's the cutest little thing," but it came out "coot"—and the name stuck.

I was very religious. Annie and I played church together out behind her house, setting up chairs and doing services. Her brother would be the pastor, or she would be since she was older. I'd be the shouter. The second Sunday of every month the Reverend H. H. Johnson came out from Montgomery and pastored a service at our little church in the country. We'd call it Big Meeting Sunday. People would flock in from everywhere, in cars, wagons, whatever they could get to move. On a Big Meeting Sunday, we'd pull up to church at noon and wouldn't get home until dark. First there'd be regular church, then a program, then a glee club competition, then another sermon, then different choirs would sing. You'd have food all day long and come home stuffed.

I remember this one Big Meeting Sunday, I was riding on the back of the truck before the service started, to go get ice at the general store. It was about 11:00 a.m., and we passed Mr. Jones, the white man who owned our property, walking to his own church. It was hot, and he had his blazer slung over his shoulder. His Baptist church was just a short distance from the store. Forty-five minutes later we were coming back with the ice and we passed him again, walking the other way—he was already out of church! That was just one more thing that seemed different about white people. How could anyone serve God on Sunday in less than an hour?

• • •

WHEN CLAUDETTE TURNED EIGHT, Mary Ann Colvin inherited a house in Montgomery. Excited to live in a place of their own, the family loaded their belongings—including a horse named Mack—into the back of a neighbor's cattle truck and pushed off for Alabama's capital city. Their new home was a small frame house in a tiny hilltop neighborhood sandwiched between two white subdivisions on Montgomery's northeast side. King Hill, as the neighborhood was called, consisted of three unpaved streets lined with red shotgun shacks and frame houses like the Colvins'. Toilets were out-of-doors. Though King Hill had a citywide reputation as a depressed and dangerous neighborhood, the Colvins found it to be an extremely close-knit community where people knew and looked out for one another. Neighbors sat on their front porches fanning the humid air while children played in a small nearby park with a recreation center. Sad at first to leave Annie and the open countryside, Claudette soon made her peace with city life.

• • •

CLAUDETTE: I slept with Delphine in the back bedroom with our own little fireplace. She would say her prayers as fast as she could and then jump into bed, waiting for me to hurry up and finish mine. I was a serious pray-er, asking for help in this and that, and blessing about everyone I knew, but Delphine just whipped through the Lord's Prayer and jumped into bed. As soon as I got in she'd be talking and talking, asking me how to spell this word and that, and then she'd start singing songs she'd heard on the radio and twitching and squirming around with new dances. Delphine could keep me awake all night.

Going to the movies with
Jim Crow

Daddy Q.P. had his own special chair in the front room, and no one else could sit in it. He was a small man, too small for the Army they said, but he was wiry and strong and he could do anything. He had built our house in Pine Level, and there was very little he couldn't make, grow, or fix. And he was fun. On Sunday mornings I'd sit on the floor next to him and he'd read me the funnies. We had an electric fan, but we only used it on Sundays because it sucked down electricity so fast. We didn't get a TV until the bus boycott, but our radio ran off a battery that gave us about an hour at a time of a white station, WSFA. My favorite show was *Mr. Chameleon*, about this detective who worked in disguise. I listened to the *Grand Ole Opry*, too. The star of the show was Hank Williams, a famous country singer from Montgomery. When he died, his funeral drew the biggest crowd in the history of the city. Hank Williams's wife invited the black community to attend since so many of us liked his music, but Mom wouldn't let me go because the funeral was segregated.

I loved going downtown. Montgomery had stores like J. J. Newberry's and Kress's five-and-ten, which opened onto Monroe Street—the main street for black people. Out back of Kress's there was a hot dog stand. A lady who worked there and knew my dad would stack up soda crates so I could sit down while I ate hot dogs and drank my soda.

But downtown could make me very angry, too. We could shop in white stores—they'd take our money all right—but they wouldn't let us try anything on. I never went into a fitting room like white people did. The saleslady would measure me and then go get the dress or the blouse and bring it out. She'd hold it up and tell me it was a perfect fit and expect my mom to buy it. When Delphine and I needed shoes, my mom would trace the shape of our feet on a brown paper bag and we'd carry the outline to the store because we weren't allowed to try the shoes on.

You couldn't try on a hat either unless you put a stocking on your head. They said our hair was "greasy." They said it in such a degrading way; they never said "please" or asked if we minded. Once, I went into a store with my mom and saw a beautiful Easter hat I really wanted. None of the other kids had that hat. But the saleslady kept bringing out different hats. For some reason she didn't want me to have the hat I wanted. I got madder and madder. She kept saying, "Why don't you want *this* hat?" and holding up hats I didn't want. Finally, I got frustrated and answered, "Because my ears don't stick out like yours." My mom was horrified—she covered my mouth up and marched me out of the store.

Another time I had to go to the optometrist downtown. My dad and I got to the office early—I was the very first patient. There was only one chair in the waiting room. The doctor told us to leave and come back at the end of the day. I didn't understand why until I overheard my dad telling my mom about it when we got home. The optometrist wasn't gonna let me sit in that chair until all the whites had sat in it first. He knew no white patient would ever sit in a chair that he'd seen a black sit in.

There were so many places you couldn't go and so many things you couldn't do if you were black. Oak Park was the nicest park in the city, just down the hill from us, but blacks could only walk through it. If you tried to play ball or even sit down on the benches, the police would run you out.

One year we all got excited because there was going to be a rodeo with Roy Rogers and Dale Evans at the Montgomery Coliseum. They'd do one show for whites and another for blacks. My parents bought me a cowboy hat and bought cowboy boots for Delphine. Q.P. kept our horse, Mack, in a pen out back, and every day we'd brush him until he shone and we'd take turns getting rides in our new cowboy clothes. And then the word came down that Roy and Dale didn't have time to do two shows after all, so they were cutting ours. That was the South.

• • •

CLAUDETTE EXCELLED as a student in junior high even though she was younger than her classmates. Her parents bought her a dictionary of her own, giving her an advantage in classroom spelling contests. After school she usually headed for the library or, if her homework was light, to the King Hill Recreation Center, where she learned to crochet. She studied piano, too, until her mother, impatient for her favorite songs and frustrated with Claudette constantly practicing scales, stopped paying for lessons.

Late in the summer of 1952, just two weeks before Claudette was to begin her freshman year at Booker T. Washington High School, her sister Delphine came down with a fever Sunday just before church. Her temperature climbed steadily through the afternoon. By nightfall, her body was burning and the bedsheets were soaked with perspiration. Far worse, she couldn't move her

Claudette (fifth from left, back row, the tall girl smiling) developed a lifelong love of crocheting through a club that was formed at the King Hill Recreation Center

ST. JUDE HOSPITAL IN MONTGOMERY

To many blacks, the hospital where Delphine was treated was an island of kindness. St. Jude opened in 1951 as the first racially integrated hospital in the Southeast. It provided health, education, and social services to all comers, black or white. Its founder, Father Harold Purcell, was loved by many blacks. "St. Jude's was clean and easy to get to," remembers Claudette. "Father Purcell refused to put up White and Colored signs anywhere in or around the hospital, no matter what anyone said."

arms and legs to get up. The family tried everything to break her fever, but nothing worked. They rushed her to a doctor the next morning.

• • •

CLAUDETTE: Polio came down on a lot of kids that summer. It shriveled the leg of one girl in our congregation and deformed the arm of a little boy. The doctor knew what it was as soon as he saw Delphine. He sent her to St. Jude Hospital and put her in an iron lung to help her breathe. She couldn't move. All she could do was whisper through her breath, that's what my momma said. I used to go in the car with them to visit, but Mom and Q.P. made me wait outside the hospital. They didn't want me to get sick, too, and they didn't want me to see Delphine like that. Once I tried to slip inside to see my sister, but a nurse caught me and led me back out screaming. I never saw Delphine alive again after the day she left our house to go see the doctor. The next time I saw her she was dead.

After that, I began to question everything: I asked God why He didn't answer my prayers. I asked, "Why would You take my sister? Why did You say no when I asked for my sister's deliverance?" My mom disagreed with my thinking. She said, "You prayed for Delphine's deliverance? Well, let me tell you what I was prayin' for: I was praying for God to take her, because I didn't want the Devil to have the upper hand. I didn't want her to be paralyzed for the rest of her life." I said, "Mom, I would have taken care of her. I would have gone to school to be a nurse and learned to take care of her." I would've, too.

Delphine died September 5, 1952. It was my thirteenth birthday.

Hot comb and hair-straightening products
typical of the 1950s, when Claudette attended
Booker T. Washington High School

CHAPTER THREE

"We Seemed to Hate Ourselves"

"Radical" simply means "grasping things at the root."
—Angela Davis

CLAUDETTE LEFT HER HOUSE on the first day of high school determined to put her mind on her studies. Delphine's funeral—just two weeks before—had been as sad and bewildering a day as she could remember, but now she hoped she could put it behind her. Now it was time to focus.

Booker T. Washington High, whose sports teams were known as the Yellow Jackets, was one of Montgomery's two public high schools for black students, the other being George Washington Carver High. Almost all the sons and daughters of Montgomery's working-class black families went to either Washington or Carver, with a few Catholic students attending St. Jude's and many of the children of Montgomery's black professionals enrolled at other private schools.

Booker T. Washington High was a buff-colored, three-story brick citadel. The glass in the lower windows was painted white so students couldn't look out at the street. Desktops were gouged and book covers cracked. Pages were torn from years of use. There was so little money from city funds that each year the principal put on a fund-raising event to buy desks, books, and equipment for the cafeteria. In the fall of 1952, the air around the building was thick with the dust of construction, as workers raced to complete a new wing to the school before winter in an effort to keep up with Montgomery's expanding black population.

Though being smart was an asset, Claudette soon found that having light skin and straight hair was the surest key to popularity at Booker T. Washington. Many girls woke up early and spent hours applying hot combs to their hair, trying to straighten it to look, as some said, "almost white." But Claudette's hair wouldn't stay straight or flat no matter how long she pressed it, and her skin was very dark. On top of that, she was from King Hill,

Claudette in 1952, age twelve

a neighborhood she loved but others scorned. And no matter how hard she fought it, Delphine's death had left her feeling raw and lonely, especially when she passed the spot each day where her sister had always waited for her after school. Suddenly alone, Claudette started life as a Yellow Jacket feeling she was at the very bottom of the social heap.

• • •

CLAUDETTE: Right after Delphine died, I became very sensitive. Just about any cruel word or insult could start me crying, even if it was aimed at someone besides me. One thing especially bothered me—we black students constantly put ourselves down. If you were dark-complexioned they'd call you "nappy-headed." Not "nappy-haired." Nappy-headed. And the "N" word—we were saying it to each other, to *ourselves*. I'd hear that word and I would start crying. I wouldn't let people use it around me. How could you hear such things and not feel emotional? When girls said things like that, it was bad enough, but when boys said them to you, it really hurt.

For some reason we seemed to hate ourselves. We students put down our hair texture and skin color all the time. Can you imagine getting up in the morning every day and looking in the mirror and saying to yourself, "I have bad hair"? Or "I'm black and nobody likes me"? The football players went for the girls with flowing hair and lighter skin. And who could grow wavy, shoulder-length hair? It'd be a biracial kid. The girls with the darkest complexions never got picked to be queen of anything. Middle-class black girls would always try to separate themselves from dark-skinned girls like me and emulate white girls.

• • •

TRAGEDY STRUCK ONCE AGAIN in November, when Claudette's schoolmate and neighbor, sixteen-year-old Jeremiah Reeves, was arrested and charged with raping a white housewife. Reeves confessed to the crime. Police quickly expanded the charges, claiming that he was responsible for raping six white women after breaking into their homes. Blacks in Montgomery were furious. Most were convinced that the police had forced him to confess. "One of the authorities had led him to the death chamber, threatening that if he did not confess at once he would burn there later," Martin Luther King, Jr., then the new pastor at the Dexter Avenue Baptist Church, wrote.

After a brief trial, an all-white jury sentenced Reeves to death in the electric chair. This brought blacks throughout Alabama to a boiling point. Even if Reeves was guilty of the charges—something few blacks believed—he hadn't killed anyone. Why should he pay with his life? Blacks knew that no white man accused of a similar crime against a black woman would have been convicted at all, let alone sentenced to die.

The verdict radicalized many students at Booker T. Washington High. Reeves was a popular senior, widely admired as a talented drummer. He hadn't fled from the police—in fact, he had turned himself in. Everyone

THE NAACP

The National Association for the Advancement of Colored People was formed in 1909 in New York City by a group of black and white citizens fighting for social justice. Ever since, the NAACP has organized demonstrations, pickets, and legal actions to expand and defend the rights of people of color. Many cities and communities have local NAACP chapters, including the Montgomery Chapter, which provided support to Jeremiah Reeves.

Jeremiah Reeves, with poems
he wrote in prison

had always predicted Jeremiah Reeves would go somewhere special. Now he wasn't going anywhere at all. Unless something could be done, he would languish on death row until he turned twenty-one and became legally old enough to take the short walk from his cell to the electric chair.

Jeremiah's plight pulled Claudette's attention away from her personal difficulties to the injustices blacks faced everywhere. She went to rallies, wrote letters to him in prison, and collected money for his legal defense. The effort to support Jeremiah Reeves became the first time many black teenagers in Montgomery ever acted to address injustices outside their own personal problems. Claudette Colvin was one of those teens.

• • •

CLAUDETTE: Jeremiah Reeves's arrest was the turning point of my life. That was when I and a lot of other students really started thinking about prejudice and racism. I was furious when I found out what had happened. Jeremiah lived right below us on the Hill. I knew him well, and admired him like everybody else did. We girls thought he was like a rock star because he was so stylish. He always wore a starched clean shirt, and there was never a spot of mud on his shoes. He was a wonderful drummer in the school band and in bands around town.

The NAACP was called in to take his case. That was the first time I had ever heard of them. I think that's why the jury sentenced him to death—to show that the NAACP couldn't take over the South. Everyone talked about Jeremiah Reeves at school. There were rumors that the jailers pulled out his fingernails and tortured him. One girl hid in a delivery truck and got into the jail but didn't make it to his cell. We showed movies to try to raise money for his lawyers. I would take whatever we raised to his mother.

The hypocrisy of it made me so angry! Black girls were extremely vulnerable. My mother and my grandmother told me never to go anywhere with a white man no matter what. I grew up hearing horror story after horror story about black girls who were raped by white men, and how they never got justice either. When a white man raped a black girl—something that happened all the time—it was just his word against hers, and no one would ever believe her. The white man always got off. But now they were going to hold Jeremiah for years as a minor just so they could legally

ONE GIRL'S MEMORY OF JEREMIAH REEVES

One friend and classmate of Claudette's was especially active in Jeremiah Reeves's defense. After an exchange of letters, Reeves invited the girl to visit him on death row, along with his parents. Later she remembered what it was like:

To reach death row you had to be escorted by a guard through several halls one by one. You'd step in one room and the guard would slam the door loud behind you and turn the key. Then you'd go to the next room. Finally you walked out in the backyard and up a flight of steps. At that point you passed right by the electric chair. I saw it. I'll never forget the sight of it.

Jeremiah was eighteen or nineteen when I saw him in prison. He was a fine-looking young man in good health. He hadn't been tortured. He and three other prisoners had formed a quartet on death row. They couldn't see each other through the walls but they could hear. Someone would sing a note and they would start in. His voice was rich and beautiful; they sang spirituals.

Jeremiah was a very spiritual person. Very caring. Again and again he told me he believed he would get out someday.

execute him when he came of age. That changed me. That put a lot of anger in me. I stayed angry about Jeremiah Reeves for a long time.

• • •

IN 1954, the U.S. Supreme Court threw out Reeves's conviction and ordered a new trial. (By then, Reeves had retracted his confession, insisting he had been forced by police to make it. For the rest of his life he maintained he was innocent.) But after two days' testimony, the new jury—again entirely white—took only thirty-four minutes to restore Reeves's death sentence. Now all hope was gone.

Many at school wept for their classmate, but Claudette fumed. Why did everyone accept injustice? How could adults complain at home about the insulting way they were treated at work and then put on a happy face for their white employers? Why did her classmates worry about "good hair" when they had no rights? When was anybody ever going to stand up? Claudette was still furious about Jeremiah Reeves's plight when, on the first day of her sophomore year, she met someone who gave her the confidence to transform her anger into action.

• • •

CLAUDETTE: Miss Geraldine Nesbitt dressed sharp—more like a saleslady than a schoolteacher. She was slender and petite. She grew up in Montgomery and went to Alabama State College, but she had a master's degree in education from Columbia University in New York City. She came to school early and stayed late. She was tough, but she was out to make you learn.

Geraldine Nesbitt, Claudette's favorite teacher

We were supposed to be an English literature class, but Miss Nesbitt used literature to teach life. She said she didn't have time to teach us like a regular English teacher—we were too far behind. Instead, she taught us the world through literature. She taught the Constitution. She taught the Magna Carta and the Articles of Confederation. We studied Hawthorne and Poe. We discussed Patrick Henry's speech—"Give me liberty or give me death"—and applied it to our own situation. We'd pick out a passage from the Bible and examine it from a literary standpoint. We wrote poems and essays and themes. We even wrote obituaries.

She brought in her own books from home, because we had so few books in our library at school. One day we all came into class and Miss Nesbitt had her face buried in an open book. We all said, "Why are you doing that?" Finally she came up with a big smile and said, "Ahhhh . . . there's no smell as good as the smell of a new book."

Right at the end of sophomore year, the Supreme Court ruled that public schools like ours would have to be integrated, though they didn't say when. Whenever it happened, it was bound to be a big change. Segregation was so total. It wasn't just that we went to separate schools: we even walked to school on opposite sides of the highway from whites, shouting insults at each other across the street. In class we asked each other, "Would you want to sit next to a white student?" A lot of kids said things like "If they don't want to sit next to me on a bus, why would I want to sit next to one in class?"

I felt differently. I wanted to go to college. I wanted to grow up and greet the world, and so did my best friends. I thought if whites came into our schools, maybe our textbooks would improve. Sometimes when I babysat I'd sneak looks at the textbooks of white students who lived in those families. There were essays on the Lincoln-Douglas debate, which I had never heard of. They made me think for the first time about the economic basis for slavery. While we were taking routine math, whites my age were studying algebra. Our school's entire set of encyclopedias only had two articles about blacks—Booker T. Washington and George Washington Carver. In fact, we had very few books of any kind in our school library, and the library downtown—the "colored" library—didn't have many more. I didn't care who I sat next to. I wanted a good education.

Miss Nesbitt made us see that we had a history, too—that our story didn't begin by being captured and chained and thrown onto a boat. There had been life and culture before that. She related literature back to our lives. She would ask, "Why do we celebrate the Fourth of July—

The children involved in the landmark civil rights lawsuit *Brown v. Board of Education*, which challenged segregation in public schools, in Topeka, Kansas, 1953: (left to right) Vicki Henderson, Donald Henderson, Linda Brown (the Brown of the case's name), James Emanuel, Nancy Todd, and Katherine Carper

Independence Day—when we are still in slavery?" "Why are there no black people except Sammy Davis, Jr., and Pearl Bailey on TV?"

I had Miss Nesbitt in both tenth and eleventh grades, and during those years I grew in confidence. In those two years she challenged many assumptions I had taken for granted. She said, "There's no such thing as 'good hair'—hair is just hair. Everyone is born with the hair they have and you just do the best you can with it." Same with skin color. She wanted us to love whatever color we were. Our history teacher, Miss Josie Lawrence, was the blackest teacher in the whole school, but she had the same attitude. She'd say, "I'm a real African. I'm a pure-blooded African." She was proud of it.

She taught us all the different nations of Africa and the periods of African history. It all made sense to me. I wasn't ashamed of my thick lips and broad nose and coarse hair. I had always thought God made our features so we could be comfortable in the hot African sun.

Little by little, I began to form a mission for myself. I was going be like Harriet Tubman and go North to liberate my people. I admired Harriet Tubman more than anyone else I read about—her courage, the pistol she wore, the fact that she never lost a passenger on the Underground Railroad. I wasn't going to go to Alabama State College, where they taught you how to teach school but didn't teach you how to get your freedom.

We had nothing but preachers and teachers in the South. I was going to do something different. I was going to be a lawyer. My mom always said I could outtalk any forty lawyers—I agreed it would be a good fit.

In 1955, my junior year, Miss Nesbitt and Miss Lawrence team-taught Negro History Week. We really got into it. We spent that whole February talking about the injustices we black people suffered every day in Montgomery—it was total immersion. My parents had only gone to sixth grade—they'd never had a chance for a class discussion like that. So I was grateful for it, and totally receptive. I was done talking about "good hair" and "good skin" but not addressing our grievances. I was tired of adults complaining about how badly they were treated and not doing anything about it. I'd had enough of just feeling angry about Jeremiah Reeves. I was tired of hoping for justice.

When my moment came, I was ready.

BROWN V. BOARD OF EDUCATION OF TOPEKA

Linda Brown was a third-grade student who lived in Topeka, Kansas. She had to walk five long blocks to her school every day, even though she lived much closer to a school for whites only. Linda's father sued the city government to let her go to the all-white school. The case was combined with several similar cases around the country, and it was argued all the way up to the U.S. Supreme Court, under the title *Brown v. Board of Education of Topeka*.

Lawyers from the NAACP represented Linda and the other black students. On May 17, 1954, the Supreme Court ruled 9–0 that segregated schools did not give black students an equal chance for a good education. Chief Justice Earl Warren wrote on behalf of the nine justices: "We conclude, unanimously, that in the field of public education the doctrine of 'separate but equal' has no place. Separate educational facilities are inherently unequal." Some school systems integrated smoothly, but other communities took as long as twenty years to open the school doors to all students.

A Birmingham, Alabama, city bus.
Two separate worlds within one vehicle

CHAPTER FOUR

"IT'S MY CONSTITUTIONAL RIGHT!"

Early in life, I had learned that if you want something,
you had better make some noise.
—Malcolm X

March 2, 1955

CLAUDETTE AND HER CLASSMATES got out of school early that Wednesday because of a faculty meeting. When she stepped outside, the afternoon air was warm and muggy, already like summer. Claudette spotted some friends and ran to catch up with them. The group walked together for a few blocks, then got on the Highland Gardens bus at Dexter Avenue and Bainbridge Street. She handed the driver her pink coupon, which allowed a student to ride for five cents—half fare. Since there were no whites in the front of the bus, she and her classmates walked straight down the aisle without getting off.

Claudette slid into a window seat on the left side, near the exit door and about halfway back. A schoolmate plopped down beside her, and two other Booker T. Washington students took the seats across the aisle in the same row. Balancing her textbooks on her lap, Claudette settled back and gazed absently out the window as the bus pulled away from the curb.

As the bus moved east along Dexter Avenue, the seats filled up block by block with white passengers getting off work from the downtown stores and offices. The ten front seats went quickly, and soon riders were standing in the aisle, keeping their balance by clutching poles as the bus stopped and started. Just before they reached Court Square, Claudette realized that a white woman was standing in the aisle between the four seats in her row. Clearly the woman expected Claudette and her three schoolmates to vacate the entire row so she could sit down in one of the seats.

• • •

CLAUDETTE: The motorman looked up in his mirror and said, "I need those seats." I might have considered getting up if the woman had been elderly, but she wasn't. She looked about forty. The other three girls in my row got up and moved back, but I didn't. I just couldn't.

Rebellion was on my mind that day. All during February we'd been talking about people who had taken stands. We had been studying the Constitution in Miss Nesbitt's class. I knew I had rights. I had paid my fare the same as white passengers. I knew the rule—that you didn't have to get up for a white person if there were no empty seats left on the bus—and there weren't. But it wasn't about that. I was thinking, Why should I have to get up just because a driver tells me to, or just because I'm black? Right then, I decided I wasn't gonna take it anymore. I hadn't planned it out, but my decision was built on a lifetime of nasty experiences.

After the other students got up, there were three empty seats in my row, but that white woman still wouldn't sit down—not even across the aisle from me. That was the whole point of the segregation rules—it was all symbolic—blacks had to be *behind* whites. If she sat down in the same row as me, it meant I was as good as her. So she had to keep standing until I moved back. The motorman yelled again, louder: "Why are you still sittin' there?" I didn't get up, and I didn't answer him. It got real quiet on the bus. A white rider yelled from the front, "You got to get up!" A girl named Margaret Johnson answered from the back, "She ain't got to do nothin' but stay black and die."

The white woman kept standing over my seat. The driver shouted, "Gimme that seat!" then "Get up, gal!" I stayed in my seat, and I didn't say a word.

• • •

EXASPERATED BY CLAUDETTE'S NONRESPONSE, the driver pushed on to Court Square, Montgomery's major downtown transfer station for city buses. In the late afternoon rush hour, scores of weary passengers were lined up behind signs reading "Colored" and "White."

At Court Square, the driver snapped open the doors and hollered for a transit policeman to come inside and make an arrest. Seconds later, a uniformed officer clambered aboard and the driver pointed down the aisle at Claudette. "It's her," he said.

During these moments as the bus idled, several passengers boarded through the rear door. One, a pregnant woman whom Claudette recognized as her neighbor Mrs. Hamilton, sat down heavily in the empty seat next to Claudette. Of course, Mrs. Hamilton was totally unaware of the standoff between Claudette and the driver. All she knew was that for some reason a policeman was coming her way. When he arrived, the officer saw

COURT SQUARE

If the historical importance of places could be detected by an instrument like a Geiger counter, Court Square would send the needle dancing.

At Court Square, six downtown Montgomery streets converge around a fountain topped by a statue of Hebe, goddess of youth and cupbearer to the gods. In the early 1800s, Court Square was the site of a major auction block, where livestock, furniture, and Negro slaves of all ages were exhibited and sold. Looking down Dexter Avenue from the fountain, one has a straight sight line to the Alabama State Capitol, where, in 1861, Jefferson Davis was sworn in as the first president of the Confederate States of America. To the viewer's right is the Winter Building, where, on April 10, 1861, a local boy delivered a telegram from Jefferson Davis instructing Confederate troops to start shelling Fort Sumter, South Carolina. The message touched off the Civil War.

Court Square is also within sight of the Dexter Avenue Baptist Church, pastored by Dr. Martin Luther King, Jr., from 1954 to 1960. And Court Square, as the major transfer point for City Lines buses, figured centrally in the Montgomery bus protests.

(Front of bus)

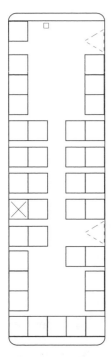

The X on this diagram indicates where Claudette was sitting on the Highland Gardens bus when she was arrested

that now there were two blacks seated in the disputed row. He ordered both women to rise. Mrs. Hamilton replied that she didn't feel like getting up. Claudette also refused.

All eyes turned to the policeman. As much as he might have wanted to evict Claudette, he hesitated to bully a pregnant woman. Cocking a thumb toward Mrs. Hamilton, he addressed a group of black men seated in the rear. "If any of you are not gentleman enough to give this lady a seat," he said, "you should be put in jail yourselves." Two men rose and scrambled off the trouble-filled bus. Mrs. Hamilton slowly walked back and took one of their seats. Now Claudette was again alone in her row.

The officer ordered her to get up. Again Claudette refused. He returned to the driver and explained that as a transit policeman he lacked the authority to make an arrest. The doors closed behind him as he stepped down into the street and the bus pulled away again. One block north, at the intersection of Bibb and Commerce streets, a squad car was waiting. This time, when the Highland Gardens bus door opened, two Montgomery city policemen climbed aboard. Passengers held their breath.

• • •

CLAUDETTE: One of them said to the driver in a very angry tone, "Who is it?" The motorman pointed at me. I heard him say, "That's nothing new . . . I've had trouble with that 'thing' before." He called me a "thing." They came to me and stood over me and one said, "Aren't you going to get up?" I said, "No, sir." He shouted "Get up" again. I started crying, but I felt even more defiant. I kept saying over and over, in my high-pitched voice, "It's my constitutional right to sit here as much as that lady. I paid my fare, it's my constitutional right!" I knew I was talking back to a white policeman, but I had had enough.

The police report that was filed when Claudette was arrested on March 2, 1955, and her fingerprint record

One cop grabbed one of my hands and his partner grabbed the other and they pulled me straight up out of my seat. My books went flying everywhere. I went limp as a baby—I was too smart to fight back. They started dragging me backwards off the bus. One of them kicked me. I might have scratched one of them because I had long nails, but I sure didn't fight back. I kept screaming over and over, "It's my constitutional right!" I wasn't shouting anything profane—I never swore, not then, not ever. I was shouting out my rights.

It just killed me to leave the bus. I hated to give that white woman my seat when so many black people were standing. I was crying hard. The cops put me in the back of a police car and shut the door. They stood outside and talked to each other for a minute, and then one came back and told me to stick my hands out the open window. He handcuffed me and then pulled the door open and jumped in the backseat with me. I put my knees together and crossed my hands over my lap and started praying.

All ride long they swore at me and ridiculed me. They took turns trying to guess my bra size. They called me "nigger bitch" and cracked jokes about parts of my body. I recited the Lord's Prayer and the Twenty-third Psalm over and over in my head, trying to push back the fear. I assumed they were taking me to juvenile court because I was only fifteen. I was thinking, Now I'm gonna be picking cotton, since that's how they punished juveniles—they put you in a school out in the country where they made you do field work during the day.

But we were going in the wrong direction. They kept telling me I was going to Atmore, the women's penitentiary. Instead, we pulled up to the police station and they led me inside. More cops looked up when we came in and started calling me "Thing" and "Whore." They booked me and took my fingerprints.

Then they put me back in the car and drove me to the city jail—the adult jail. Someone led me straight to a cell without giving me any chance to make a phone call. He opened the door and told me to get inside. He shut it hard behind me and turned the key. The lock fell into place with a heavy sound. It was the worst sound I ever heard. It sounded final. It said I was trapped.

When he went away, I looked around me: three bare walls, a toilet, and a cot. Then I fell down on my knees in the middle of the cell and started crying again. I didn't know if anyone knew where I was or what had happened to me. I had no idea how long I would be there. I cried and I put my hands together and prayed like I had never prayed before.

• • •

MEANWHILE, schoolmates who had been on the bus had run home and telephoned Claudette's mother at the house where she worked as a maid. Girls went over and took care of the lady's three small children so that Claudette's mother could leave. Mary Ann Colvin called Claudette's pastor, the Reverend H. H. Johnson. He had a car, and together they sped to the police station.

• • •

CLAUDETTE: When they led Mom back, there I was in a cell. I was cryin' hard, and then Mom got upset, too. When she saw me, she didn't bawl me out, she just asked, "Are you all right, Claudette?"

Reverend Johnson bailed me out and we drove home. By the time we got to King Hill, word had spread everywhere. All our neighbors came around, and they were just squeezing me to death. I felt happy and proud. I had been talking about getting our rights ever since Jeremiah Reeves was arrested, and now they knew I was serious. Velma, Q.P. and Mary Ann's daughter, who was living with us at the time, kept saying it was my little squeaky voice that had saved me from getting beat up or raped by the cops.

But I was afraid that night, too. I had stood up to a white bus driver and two white cops. I had challenged the bus law. There had been lynchings and cross burnings for that kind of thing. Wetumpka Highway that led out of Montgomery ran right past our house. It would have been easy for the Klan to come up the hill in the night. Dad sat up all night long with his shotgun. We all stayed up. The neighbors facing the highway kept watch. Probably nobody on King Hill slept that night.

But worried or not, I felt proud. I had stood up for our rights. I had done something a lot of adults hadn't done. On the ride home from jail, coming over the viaduct, Reverend Johnson said something to me I'll never forget. He was an adult who everyone respected and his opinion meant a lot to me. "Claudette," he said, "I'm so proud of you. Everyone prays for freedom. We've all been praying and praying. But you're different—you want your answer the next morning. And I think you just brought the revolution to Montgomery."

This school photo of Claudette was probably taken in 1953, when she was thirteen

CHAPTER FIVE

"There's the Girl Who Got Arrested"

The world is a severe schoolmaster.
—Phillis Wheatley, the first published African-American poet (1753?–1784)

THE NEWS that a schoolgirl had been arrested for refusing to surrender her bus seat to a white passenger flashed through Montgomery's black community and traveled far beyond. One man from Sacramento, California, wrote to Claudette:

> The wonderful thing which you have just done makes me feel like a craven coward. How encouraging it would be if more adults had your courage, self-respect and integrity.

In Montgomery, students stopped one another at bus corners and by their lockers, saying things like "Have you ever heard of Claudette Colvin?" "Well, do you *know* anyone who knows her?" "Where's she go to school?"

Jo Ann Robinson, a professor of English at Alabama State College at the time, later wrote, "[With]in a few hours, every Negro youngster on the streets discussed Colvin's arrest. Telephones rang. Clubs called special meetings and discussed the event with some degree of alarm. Mothers expressed concern about permitting their children on the buses."

Jo Ann Robinson had a personal reason to admire anyone who took on the bus system. In 1949, just after she had moved to Montgomery, Robinson had boarded a bus for the airport. It was Christmas break, and she was flying off to Cleveland to visit relatives. After dropping a dime in the fare box, she absentmindedly sat down in one of the ten front seats reserved for whites. Still new to town, she hadn't thought to walk to the back. Besides, there were only two other passengers on the entire bus. Lost in holiday thoughts, she was startled by the realization that someone's face was inches from hers. It was the bus driver, shouting, "Get up from there! Get up from there!" His hand was drawn back as if to strike her. She snatched up her packages and stumbled out the front door, nearly sprawling in the mud as the bus pulled away. "I felt like a dog," she later wrote.

He had picked the wrong person to bully. Smart, energetic, and extremely well-connected, Jo Ann Robinson was an active member of the Women's Political Council, a large and influential civic group of professional black women in Montgomery. Some WPC members were Alabama State College professors; others, including Claudette's teacher, Geraldine Nesbitt, were ASC graduates who had become teachers. Shortly after Robinson took over as president of the WPC in 1950, she led a successful campaign to make white merchants include the titles "Mr.," "Mrs.," and "Miss" on bills and announcements sent to black customers. It was an important measure of respect.

Jo Ann Robinson, professor of English at Alabama State College and leader of Montgomery's influential Women's Political Council

Though Robinson owned her own car and rarely rode the city bus, the memory of the driver's bullying behavior and how humiliated she had felt wouldn't go away. She started interviewing black residents

BUS BOYCOTTS

The idea of boycotting—or staying off—public vehicles until reforms were made was nothing new, but it had never succeeded for long on a large scale. Between 1900 and 1906, Montgomery was one of twenty-five Southern cities to protest segregated streetcars through boycotts. More recently, in June 1953, the black community of Baton Rouge, Louisiana, had boycotted the city's buses for several days to protest segregated seating. Though they weren't able to evict Jim Crow, the Baton Rouge protesters developed a free-ride transportation system and left a detailed blueprint for other bus protesters to follow.

who had been mistreated on the city buses and writing down their stories. She soon possessed a thick file of nightmare accounts.

Robinson longed to do something about the buses, but she didn't know quite what. In March 1954, she organized a face-to-face meeting of black leaders, city officials, and bus company representatives to complain about the way blacks were treated on the buses and to propose reforms. The meeting was pleasant enough but unproductive.

She kept at it. Two months later she wrote a letter to Montgomery's mayor, W. A. "Tacky" Gayle, on behalf of the Women's Political Council. Robinson pressed for three changes to the bus rules:

1. A new seating plan that would let blacks sit from back to front and whites from front to back until the bus filled up, as was the practice in several other Southern cities.

2. An end to making blacks pay their fares at the front of the bus but then get off and reenter through the rear door to find a seat at the back.

3. A requirement that drivers stop at every corner in black neighborhoods just as they did in white neighborhoods.

Robinson's diplomatic letter contained one fragment of steel. In the third to last paragraph she wrote that, if things did not get better, "there has been talk from twenty-five or more local organizations of planning a city-wide boycott of busses."

The idea of a bus boycott had been gaining momentum throughout the black community for months. Its power was obvious: three-quarters of Montgomery's bus passengers were black. If everyone quit riding, they could *starve* the City Lines bus company into reason. Still, the letter stopped short of calling for an end to segregated seating. As Robinson later wrote, "In Montgomery in 1955 no one was brazen enough to announce publicly that black people might boycott City buses for the specific purpose of integrating those buses. Just to say that minorities wanted 'better seating arrangements' was bad enough."

Robinson's letter led only to more polite meetings. The whites offered coffee, nodded, and smiled, but refused to budge an inch when it came to Jim Crow. Still, Claudette Colvin's arrest had stripped the veneer of politeness from the talks. She had been wrenched from her seat and dragged off a bus by police in front of shocked witnesses. People were angry.

Claudette's arrest made her the center of attention wherever she went. On the following Sunday, Reverend Johnson led the congregation in prayer for the girl among them who had been arrested for bravely standing up to the bus driver and the police and challenging the whole ugly system. The next day classmates swarmed around her when she pulled up to Booker T. Washington High School in her cousin's car. They followed her into homeroom and asked to hear her story. Students pointed at her in the halls, whispering, "There's the girl who got arrested."

Opinion at Booker T. Washington was sharply divided between those who admired Claudette's courage and those who thought she got what she deserved for making things harder for everyone. Some said it was about time someone stood up. Others told her that if she didn't like the way things were in the South, she should go up North. Still others couldn't make up their minds: no one they knew had ever done anything like this before.

"A few of the teachers like Miss Nesbitt embraced me," Claudette recalls. "They kept saying, 'You were so brave.' But other teachers seemed uncomfortable. Some parents seemed uncomfortable, too. I think they knew they should have done what I did long before. They were embarrassed that it took a teenager to do it."

Facing serious criminal charges, and with her court hearing only two weeks away, Claudette feared she might be sent to a reform school as a juvenile delinquent. She had a lot to lose: she was a good student with dreams of college and a career. She was not about to plead guilty to anything, but she didn't know what to do or whom to turn to. Somehow, she had to find a lawyer, and figure out how to pay for one. She had no time to lose.

• • •

CLAUDETTE: Everybody got busy. We started working family connections, trying to find someone to help me. My great-aunt's husband, C. J. McNear, told my parents to get in touch with Mr. E. D. Nixon. C.J. thought my case might be a good civil rights case. Mr. Nixon called the shots in the black community of Montgomery. He knew everybody. So Mom called him. And he agreed to help us.

Plainspoken E. D. Nixon, longtime leader of the Montgomery NAACP

• • •

NIXON MOVED SWIFTLY on two fronts. He called Fred Gray,

E. D. NIXON

When black people had serious problems in Montgomery, they went to E. D. Nixon. Employed as a railroad sleeping car porter, Nixon worked tirelessly throughout his life to advance the rights of black people. A tall, rugged man with a commanding voice and an earthy sense of humor, Nixon seemed to know everyone: jailers, white policemen, judges, newspaper reporters, lawyers, and government officials. An early president of the Montgomery Chapter of the NAACP, Nixon was often able to fix common people's problems through plain talk and informal dealing before they hardened into legal cases.

one of Montgomery's two black lawyers, and convinced him to represent Claudette in court. Then he organized a committee of black leaders to meet downtown with the police commissioner. Among those selected was the new pastor of the Dexter Avenue Baptist Church, twenty-six-year-old Dr. Martin Luther King, Jr. The attempt to obtain justice for Claudette Colvin marked Dr. King's political debut.

A conference of black leaders, the bus company's manager, and the police commissioner seemed to break the tension. "Both men were quite pleasant, and expressed deep concern over what had happened [to Claudette]," Dr. King later wrote. The bus company conceded that, according to the driver, Claudette had been sitting behind the ten white seats in front and there had been no seats available when the driver ordered her to move. That seemed to be an admission that she hadn't broken the law. The police commissioner agreed the seating rules were confusing and promised that the city's attorney would soon clarify them in writing. The one thing they didn't do was drop the charges against Claudette. The trial would go on.

Still, Dr. King walked out of the meeting feeling "hopeful," and Jo Ann Robinson also felt her spirits lifting as she stepped outside. "[We] were given to understand . . . that . . . Claudette would be given every chance to clear her name," she later wrote. "It was not [to be] a trial to determine guilt or innocence, but an effort to find out the truth, and if the girl were found innocent, her record would be clear . . . Those present left the conference feeling . . . that everything would work out fairly for everyone."

In the days before Claudette's trial, E. D. Nixon also called Rosa Parks, a soft-spoken, forty-two-year-old professional seamstress who had for many years been secretary of the Montgomery NAACP. Mrs. Parks was also the head of the NAACP's youth group in Montgomery. Nixon and Mrs. Parks had long tried to get more young blacks involved in the struggle for civil rights, but the Sunday afternoon NAACP youth meetings were, for the most part, poorly attended. However, both saw promise in the dramatic arrest, jailing, and trial of a fifteen-year-old bus protester. It might spark interest if the girl was willing to tell her story. Nixon urged Mrs. Parks to get Claudette Colvin involved with the NAACP.

• • •

CLAUDETTE: The first time I ever met Rosa Parks was one Sunday afternoon when she walked into a church before an NAACP youth meeting. There were only a few students around. This small, fair-skinned woman with long, straight hair came up to me, and looked me up and down. She said, "You're Claudette Colvin? Oh my God, I was lookin' for some big old burly overgrown teenager who sassed white people out . . . But no, they pulled a little girl off the bus." I said, "They pulled me off because I refused to walk off."

Rosa had already asked the teachers at my school about me and found out I was a good student. She got even more interested when she realized she knew my mother—my biological mom—from Pine Level. Rosa had lived there, too, when she was younger. Mom was close friends with Rosa's brother, Sylvester, before she left Pine Level for Birmingham.

We did all sorts of things to raise money for my lawyer. Rosa's mother

Rosa Parks worked as a department store seamstress and served for many years as the secretary of Montgomery's branch of the NAACP. Pleasant and soft-spoken, she was a steely foe of racial segregation.

baked and sold cookies. I was always eating them, and Rosa would come up and say, "Claudette, don't eat all the cookies or we won't have any to sell." Rosa put me up for Miss NAACP, Montgomery Chapter. I finished second, but it didn't matter; all the money from the contest went to pay my lawyer anyway.

• • •

CLAUDETTE'S LAWYER wasn't much older than she was. Bespectacled, serious, sporting a pencil-thin mustache, and usually seen in a neatly pressed suit, twenty-four-year-old Fred Gray was just

Claudette's lawyer, Fred Gray— young, smart, and "determined to destroy everything segregated I could find"

six months out of law school in March 1955. The youngest of five children, he had grown up riding the Montgomery city buses in a triangle between school and home and his job with a newspaper. He had never himself been beaten or threatened on a bus, but he had heard more than enough insults and witnessed more than enough abuse of black passengers to last a lifetime. Like Claudette, he had vowed to study law in the North and then return home to "destroy everything segregated I could find."

After high school, Gray worked his way rapidly through Alabama State College and then went off to law school in Ohio. True to his pledge, he returned to Montgomery soon after graduation, passed the Alabama bar exam, and opened his practice in a tiny downtown office, finding his first clients though black churches and NAACP meetings. He had lunch almost every day with Rosa Parks, who worked across the street at the Montgomery Fair department store. When E. D. Nixon suggested he take the Claudette Colvin case, Gray leaped at the chance. Since Claudette had been charged with breaking the city and state segregation laws, Gray hoped he could use the case to show they were unconstitutional. There had never been a chance before, since no one except Claudette Colvin had ever pleaded not guilty to breaking the segregation laws in a bus arrest.

One March evening, Gray and his secretary, Bernice Hill, drove out to King Hill to meet Claudette and her parents. They sat around the Colvins' small kitchen table sipping coffee and talking, while Hill took notes. Since Claudette was still a legal minor, one of her parents would have to file the lawsuit on her behalf. Given its importance, both parents would have to strongly support it. Gray took an instant liking to the entire family, sizing them up as brave and self-reliant. For her part, Claudette admired Fred Gray as the first person she had ever met who was doing what she herself wanted to do someday.

Gray urged all three to consider the hazards of contesting the charges in court. By pleading not guilty, Claudette would be doing more than just talking back to whites: she would be challenging Jim Crow dead-on. Her name would almost certainly be in the paper. Homes had been bombed, jobs lost, and people lynched for less. All three Colvins simply looked back at him, unshaken. Gray turned to Claudette and asked if she was sure.

"Yes, I am," she replied.

Her quick response and the family's unity of purpose sent Fred Gray off King Hill with a sense of hope. Whatever was to come, at least the Colvins were not people who would back down.

There had been thirteen black students on the Highland Gardens bus the day Claudette was arrested, most of them her classmates at Booker T. Washington. Gray arranged for the high school principal to issue passes for students willing to testify at Claudette's hearing. Just before the trial, he spoke to them as a group, coaching them about what they might be asked and how best to answer.

In the days before Claudette's hearing, black leaders rallied around her. The Citizens Coordinating Committee, a group of prominent black men and women, mimeographed a leaflet and passed it around Montgomery. Entitled "To Friends of Justice and Human Rights," it described Claudette's arrest and demanded that she be acquitted of charges. It also called for punishment of the bus driver and insisted on clarification of the long-standing city bus rule—constantly ignored by drivers—that said no rider had to give up a seat unless another was available.

Claudette's hearing was held on March 18, 1955, late in the morning. A cousin drove Claudette, Q.P., and their neighbor Annie Larkin off the Hill and down to Montgomery County's juvenile court. Claudette felt certain her troubles would be over by nightfall. "I thought Fred Gray was a very good lawyer," she remembers. "He seemed to have prepared very well. I was confident."

Because Claudette's plea of not guilty to breaking the segregation law was important to every black bus rider in Montgomery, several leaders attended the hearing, including Jo Ann Robinson and the Reverend Ralph Abernathy, pastor of the First Baptist Church. It was nearly noon when Claudette and Fred Gray were summoned into the small courtroom to appear before Juvenile Court Judge Wiley Hill, Jr. Students remained in the hall, straining to hear what was going on behind the door and waiting for their names to be called.

Claudette faced three separate charges: violating the segregation law, disturbing the peace, and "assaulting" one of the policemen who had pulled her off the bus. Judge Hill heard testimony from Patrolmen Paul Headley and T. J. Ward, the arresting officers. Ward testified that when he'd placed Claudette under arrest, she had "fought" the officers, kicking and scratching them. "She insisted she was colored and just as good as white," Ward informed the judge. The two officers were able to show a letter written by a white passenger on the bus that day, praising them as "gentlemen almost to the point of turning the other cheek" who spoke to Claudette in "tones so soft that I doubt if any of the other passengers aboard the bus even heard them." When called, Fred Gray's student witnesses offered a very different story, of two police officers confronting a teenage girl with frightening force on a packed bus. Gray challenged the laws themselves, contending that the provisions of Alabama's laws and Montgomery's city ordinances requiring racial segregation were unconstitutional.

Just before lunchtime, Judge Hill delivered his blunt ruling: guilty of all charges. Claudette would be placed on probation, was declared a ward of the state, and was released to the custody of her parents. He cracked his gavel, dismissing the case. As the words washed over Claudette, she felt a wave of anguish, and then everything she had been holding inside for the past two weeks came pouring out. "Claudette's agonized sobs penetrated the atmosphere of the courthouse," wrote Jo Ann Robinson. "Many people brushed away their own tears."

• • •

CLAUDETTE: Now I was a criminal. Now I would have a police record whenever I went to get a job, or when I tried to go to college. Yes, I was free on probation, but I would have to watch my step everywhere I went for at least a year. Anyone who didn't like me could get me in trouble. On top of that I hadn't done anything wrong. Not everyone knew the bus rule that said they couldn't make you get up and stand if there was no seat available for you to go to—but I did. When the driver told me to go back, there *was* no other seat. I hadn't broken the law. And assaulting a police officer? I probably wouldn't have lived for very long if I had assaulted those officers.

When I got back to school, more and more students seemed to turn against me. Everywhere I went people pointed at me and whispered. Some kids would snicker when they saw me coming down the hall. "It's my constitutional right! It's my constitutional right!" I had taken a stand for my people. I had stood up for our rights. I hadn't expected to become a hero, but I sure didn't expect this.

I cried a lot, and people saw me cry. They kept saying I was "emotional." Well, who wouldn't be emotional after something like that? Tell me, who wouldn't cry?

Negro Girl Found Guilty Of Segregation Violation

A 15-year-old Negro girl was placed on indefinite probation by Juvenile Court Judge Wiley C. Hill Jr. yesterday for violation of the city segregation law by refusing to move to the rear of a City Lines bus when requested by the driver.

Claudette Colvin of 622 E. Dixie Dr., a bespectacled, studious looking high school student, accepted the court's ruling with the same cool aloofness she had maintained throughout her 2½-hour hearing.

Appeal Is Planned

Fred D. Gray, 24-year-old Negro attorney who represented the girl, along with Negro Atty. Charles D. Langford, announced immediately after the decision he would file an appeal to circuit court.

Thetford, who served as special prosecutor, moved at the beginning of the hearing to consolidate the three charges against the girl into one. She was charged with disorderly conduct, assault and battery against Patrolman Thomas J. Ward, and violation of Chapter 6, Section 11 of the Montgomery City Code which makes it "unlawful for any passenger to refuse or fail to take a seat among those assigned to the race to which he belongs. . ."

Refused To Move

The incident occurred at the intersection of Bibb and Commerce Streets, on March 2 when the City Lines bus driver, Robert W. Cleere, requested Claudette Colvin and another Negro girl who was sitting beside her to move to the rear. The other girl heeded the request, it was brought out in testimony, but Claudette balked. She still refused after Patrolman E. R. Crew, summoned by the driver, stuck his head in the rear door of the bus and again asked her to move.

A squad car containing Patrolman Ward and Paul Headley arrived, and the girl refused a third time to move at their request. The officers then carried her from the bus. Ward said as he was putting her in the rear of the police car, the girl "hit, scratched and kicked" him. He finally got her in, he said, and Officer Headley, coming around the other side of the car, placed handcuffs on her.

Judge Hill ruled the girl "a ward of the State of Alabama and to be placed on probation pending further orders of this court." He pointed out the juvenile court could not impose a fine or a hard labor sentence but had three choices: (1) place the girl in an institution; (2) place her on probation; or (3) place her under supervision.

AU Visitors File Report

Air Force Facility Is Complimented

A complimentary report on the progress of education in the Air Force was filed yesterday by a visiting panel of educators and businessmen who completed an inspection of the Air University at Maxwell Air Force Base.

The university's board of visitors began its annual tour Monday to study methods used in indoctrinating high-ranking Air Force officers in command planning.

Board Chairman William V. Kahler, president of Illinois Bell Telephone Co., said the Air University has attained "a phenomenal character in the short span of nine years since its establishment."

Dr. Hubert E. Searcy, president of Huntingdon College, a new member of the group, said he felt "a lot better about the future of the country" after viewing the Air University facilities and training program.

Members attended the eleventh meeting of the board were Chairman Kahler; Dr. Searcy, Father John A. O'Brien, professor of philosophy, Fairfield University, (Conn.); Dr. Clifford C. Furnas, chancellor, University of Buffalo; Dr. John A. Hannah, president, Michigan State College, Dr. Frederick W. Heimberger, vice president, Ohio State University, Thomas J. Watson Jr., president, International Business Machines Crop.; Gill Robb Wilson, editor, Flying Magazine; Dr. Joseph C. Hinsey, dean, Cornell University Medical School, and Dr. Detlev W.

SMU CHOIR SCHEDULES CONCERT HERE: Methodist University Choir will give a concert Sunday at 8 p.m. in the First Methodist Church the direction of Dr. Orville J. Borchers, dean music. The choir of 40 will present some of the gre of Europe and America. The Wesley Fellowship ing the choir's performance.

State Rights Move B By Fisheries Commi

A resolution protecting states rights of aquatic nature on the Gulf of Mexico was defeated here yesterday in a closed door executive session of the Gulf States Marine Fisheries Commission.

The resolution opposed the making of "any fisheries treaty convention, compact or agreement which does not specifically provide the right of the five gulf states to regulate their aquatic resources is not limited."

Lee Eddy, chief of the Louisiana Fish and Wild Life Service, who proposed the resolution said the Marin Commissioners turned down the resolution with Alabama's commissioners splitting, Florida abstaining from voting and Texas voting no. That, he said, left only Louisiana voting for the resolution since Mississippi had no vote present at that time except the president of the commission who was not eligible to cast his ballot.

Cites Payment On Shrimp

Charles Murphy of the Louisiana Fish and Wildlife Service, a former newspaperman, said the federal

shrimp caught.

He said it v blackmail scheme government that fishing waters." plenty of fishin this sort of bl since we have o

Retaliati

Texas and Flo own waters for fear retaliation go for the resol

The resolution Eddy in an open ing but Dr. W. C Ala., proposed go into executiv The executive minutes.

Senator Herm dent of the GSM here through th ending yesterda portant session legislature.

Early yesterd of State Willia parted from Mo ing closeted wit

This newspaper article appeared in the *Alabama Journal* on March 19, 1955

CHAPTER SIX

"CRAZY" TIMES

*I had crossed the line. I was free; but there was no one to welcome
me to the land of freedom. I was a stranger in a strange land.*
—Harriet Tubman

Spring and Summer 1955

THE MORNING AFTER HER HEARING, an article about Claudette's conviction appeared in the *Montgomery Advertiser*. Headlined "Negro Guilty of Violation of City Bus Segregation Law," the story reminded readers that, according to the city code, "a bus driver has police power while in charge of a bus and must see that white and Negro passengers are segregated."

As word spread, an atmosphere of tension settled over Montgomery. "The verdict was a bombshell," Jo Ann Robinson later wrote. "Blacks were as near a breaking point as they had ever been. Resentment, rebellion and unrest were evident in all Negro circles. For a few days, large numbers refused to use the buses ... Complaints streamed in from everywhere.

"The question of boycotting came up again and loomed in the minds of thousands of black people," Robinson continued. "On paper, the Women's Political Council had already planned for fifty thousand notices calling people to boycott the buses; only the specifics of time and place had to be added ... But some members were doubtful; some wanted to wait. The women wanted to be certain the entire city was behind them, and opinions differed where Claudette was concerned. Some felt she was too young to be the trigger that precipitated the movement."

Was she too young? Could a rebellious teen be controlled? Who *was* this girl anyway? Robinson's WPC lieutenants probed into Claudette's background, since few adult leaders in Montgomery had ever heard of her. They already knew that her mother and father were not part of the elite social set that revolved around Alabama State College and the Dexter Avenue Baptist Church. Investigation showed that Claudette Colvin was being raised by her great-uncle and great-aunt, respectively a "yard boy" and a "day lady," as maids were called. The Colvins lived in King Hill, a neighborhood that meant "poor" or "inferior" to most who didn't live there. And the Hutchinson Street Baptist Church, which Claudette faithfully attended, was a church for the working poor.

This list, probably written by NAACP secretary Rosa Parks, shows contributions made by churches to "the Colvin case"

Doubts crept in. A swarm of adjectives began to buzz around Claudette Colvin, words like "emotional" and "uncontrollable" and "profane" and "feisty." The bottom line was, as Jo Ann Robinson tactfully put it, that "opinions differed where Claudette was concerned." E. D. Nixon later explained, "I had to be sure that I had somebody I could win with." So the leaders of the burgeoning Montgomery bus revolt turned away from Claudette Colvin.

About the only person not involved in these discussions was Claudette. "Nobody ever came to interview me about being a boycott

APPEALING A LEGAL DECISION

The U.S. legal system begins with city and county courts, goes on to state courts, then to federal courts, and finally to the U.S. Supreme Court. If a person does not agree with a court decision, she or he can usually appeal the case to a higher court.

It is tempting to appeal, to take a second chance. But lawyers are expensive, and winning cases on appeal is not always easy, as judges are sometimes reluctant to reverse the decisions of their colleagues on lower courts.

In Claudette's case, black leaders decided to appeal a decision made in Montgomery's juvenile court to the next level, Montgomery Circuit Court, which was still within the state of Alabama's court system.

spokesperson," she later said. "I had no idea adults were talking about me and looking into my life. The only one of those people I talked to was my lawyer, Fred Gray."

The NAACP and other Montgomery groups decided not to protest Claudette's conviction with a bus boycott, but they did raise money to appeal the ruling, partly to clear her name and partly so they could keep using her case to attack the segregation law. Leaders were eager to appeal it all the way up to federal court. Throughout March, Montgomery's black churchgoers were asked to drop a little extra into the collection plate for Claudette Colvin's case. By the end of the month, fourteen churches and four civic groups had chipped in to raise almost all of what the lawyers were charging.

Virginia Durr, a wealthy and influential white Montgomerian who supported the NAACP, launched her own support drive for Claudette. She wrote Curtis MacDougall, a college professor she knew, and asked him to persuade his students to collect money for the appeal and write Claudette messages of support. "I just can't explain how this little girl was so brave," Mrs. Durr wrote. "It was a miracle . . . Even after being deserted [on the bus] by her other companions she still *would not move*. In this setting and in this town and with *four* big burly white men threatening her—isn't that amazing?" More than one hundred letters soon arrived addressed to Claudette in care of Mrs. Rosa Parks, Secretary of the Montgomery NAACP.

On May 6, 1955, Gray went back to Montgomery Circuit Court to appeal Claudette's conviction. After hearing testimony, Judge Eugene Carter dropped two of the three charges against Claudette—disturbing the peace and breaking the segregation law. But he kept the third, her conviction for "assaulting" an officer who had lifted her out of her seat and dragged her off the bus. He sentenced Claudette to pay a small fine and kept her on probation in the custody of her parents.

It was a dispiriting outcome on two scores. First, Montgomery's black leaders had hoped to keep using Claudette's case in higher courts to challenge the constitutionality of segregated bus seating. But now that Judge Carter had shrewdly dropped that charge, there was nothing left to appeal that was specifically about segregation. All the leaders but Gray lost interest in appealing Claudette's case any further.

Second, Claudette still had a criminal record. She had been convicted of assaulting a police officer, information that would forever blemish her job applications, credit record, and school transcripts. By keeping the assault charge, Judge Carter deprived Claudette of peace of mind. Now she feared that people would see her as a juvenile delinquent, a criminal, someone with a mark against her name. Had she thrown away her dreams by taking a stand?

As cold, rainy weather set in, blacks returned to the buses. Claudette went back to school to finish out the last few weeks of her junior year. She soon found that attitudes at Booker T. Washington had hardened against her. It was easier to see the "bus girl" as a troublemaker than as a pioneer. More and more students mocked her now. Shaken, but defiant to the core, Claudette battled back—in her own way.

• • •

CLAUDETTE: One Saturday I was home by myself waiting around for an appointment with the beautician to have my hair straightened. And then it hit me: Why am I wasting my time and two good dollars straightening my hair so I can look more white? I went straight into the kitchen and washed it. Then I pulled it out into little braids while it was still damp. When I was done I looked like I was about six years old.

My mother came in the door to ask me why I didn't show up at the beauty shop. Then she took one look at my hair and said, *"What?"*

Making those pigtails was the strongest statement I could make in that school. If I had cut all my hair off, they probably would have locked me in an institution. Miss Nesbitt was right: My hair was "good hair," no matter what. By wearing it natural I was saying, "I think I'm as pretty as you are." All of a sudden it seemed such a waste of time to heat up a comb and straighten your hair before you went to school. So I just quit doing it. I felt very emotional about segregation, about the way we were treated, and about the way we treated each other. I told everybody, "I won't straighten my hair until they straighten out this mess." And that meant until we got some justice.

When I went to school the next Monday, people were cold shocked. Teachers asked me, "Why would you do such a thing?" They wouldn't let me be in the school play because of how I wore my hair. Classmates said I was still grieving Delphine. I tried to put it out of my mind, but no one else would.

At that time I had a boyfriend named Fred Harvey. He was in my homeroom and I used to help him with his homework. He was really sweet. He'd take me to the movies and save enough money so he could send me home in a taxi rather than put me on the bus. But he was just stunned. He kept asking me, "Why, why? Why won't you straighten your hair?" I told him I thought my hair looked "African," and I was proud of it. That really got him. Back then we never used the word "African." Africa was the jungle, Africa was Tarzan. We were supposed to be ashamed of our African past. But Africa made me proud. That whole spring, until school was out, just about all I heard from anybody was "You're crazy. You're crazy. You're crazy."

• • •

"**FROM THE TIME CLAUDETTE GOT ARRESTED** she was the center of attention," remembers Alean Bowser, one of Claudette's classmates. "But the attention was directed in the wrong way. Kids were saying she should have known what would happen, that she should have got up from her seat. Everything was reversed, everyone blamed her rather than the people who did those things to her. They would whisper as she went down the hall. It was mean.

"What she did with her hair just made it worse. She had always kept her hair neatly styled. And then she just came to school one day with cornrows . . . It was shocking. Kids had already pulled back from her. They were already whispering she was crazy and things like that. I was shocked, too, but I wasn't embarrassed by what she did with her hair. I was on her side. Claudette was a wonderful person, with a mind that was mature beyond her years. One day our teacher told us to write down on a piece of paper what we wanted to be when we grew up and pass it up front. Claudette wrote, 'President of the U.S.' I think she meant it. We should have been rallying around her and being proud of what she had done, but instead we ridiculed her."

School recessed for the year and the sun set about baking central Alabama. As the long, buggy summer days drifted by, Claudette spent much of her time at King Hill Park, sitting outside on the veranda, crocheting and talking to her cousin, dragging her chair around to follow the shade. Often she helped her mother take care of her white family's three young children. Every now and then she scraped up a babysitting job. Nights seemed even slower. Dances and parties were out—what if something went wrong? One false move, or one malicious report, and she was a parole violator. Claudette lost touch with her friends, stayed home, and turned inward.

At least there was still church. On Sundays after services at Hutchinson Street Baptist, she would go across town to Rosa Parks's NAACP youth meetings. Mrs. Parks had appointed Claudette youth secretary, which meant keeping attendance and membership records and putting out notices. The meetings were held at the red-brick Trinity Lutheran Church, pastored by the Reverend Robert S. Graetz. He was the only white minister in Montgomery with an all-black congregation.

• • •

CLAUDETTE: I only went if I could get a ride, because I didn't want to ride the bus anymore. If I couldn't get a ride back, I'd stay overnight at Rosa's—

she lived in the projects across the street. Rosa was hard to get to know, but her mom was just the opposite—warm and talkative and funny. We would stay up all night gabbing, sometimes while Rosa pinned wedding dresses on me that she was altering for work. Rosa's mother knew all sorts of horror stories about black girls getting mistreated. There was nothing we couldn't talk about.

Rosa Parks was like two different people inside and out of the meetings. She was very kind and thoughtful; she knew exactly how I liked my coffee and fixed me peanut butter and Ritz crackers, but she didn't say much at all. Then, when the meetings started, I'd think, Is that the same lady? She would come across very strong about rights. She would pass out leaflets saying things like "We are going to break down the walls of segregation."

I might have had more fun if the meetings had been in my neighborhood. The children in the NAACP youth group weren't like the students I went to school with. Their parents were professionals; these children went to private schools. Whenever they said they planned to go North for an education after they graduated, Rosa would scold them. "Why should your families have to send you North? Our colleges right here could offer a good education, too—but they're segregated." Rosa kept inviting me to tell my bus arrest story to the kids there, but after a while they had all heard it a million times. They seemed bored with it.

• • •

IT WAS DURING ONE OF THOSE SUMMER VISITS across town that Claudette met someone who actually listened—or seemed to. While watching a baseball game in a park, Claudette was joined by a light-skinned black man. She judged him to be maybe ten years older than she was, married, he said, but separated from his wife and living with his mother. He said he was a Korean War veteran, and backed up his claim with lively stories from places in distant parts of the world.

• • •

CLAUDETTE: I liked talking to him. He was the first person to understand my hair. Everyone else kept saying I was crazy, or "mental," but he got it. He said it was impossible for black people to have really straight hair anyway; he had seen Asian women with straight hair all the way down to their feet. No black woman could ever grow hair like that no matter how she tried. He kept telling me to ignore what people were saying about me. I really needed to hear that. He was easy to talk to. I could relate to him. I would say things like "The revolution is here—we need to stand up!" and he would agree. But all the time I knew that I was getting in over my head. He was so much older than me, and had so much more experience. I knew I was getting into a situation I couldn't handle, but it was hard to stop.

• • •

THE SLOW, SULTRY SUMMER finally came to an end when, just after Labor Day, Claudette celebrated her sixteenth birthday and returned to Booker T. Washington High for her senior year. Her legal case had died with the appeal decision, and Claudette had lost contact with all the adult black leaders except Rosa Parks. Still, riding the bus continued to anger and humiliate blacks throughout Montgomery, and impatience was mounting. Leaders such as E. D. Nixon and Jo Ann Robinson kept looking for the catalyst—the "right" person or event—that would spark citywide action.

On October 21, a second teenager, eighteen-year-old Mary Louise Smith, defied a Montgomery bus driver's command. She had left home early that morning to collect the twelve dollars owed her by the white family for whom she had worked the week before. But when she finally reached their house on the other side of town, they weren't home. Now she was out not only her wage, which her family needed, but also the twenty cents for round-trip bus fare. A week of work and a trip across town for nothing: that's what she was thinking on the bus ride home when a red-haired woman appeared in the aisle by her seat and ordered her to get up and move back.

At St. Jude School, the nuns had taught Mary Louise and her siblings to respect all people regardless of their skin color, and she did. But she was angry that day. She was thinking, It's the bus driver's job to ask, and to ask politely. Muttering a rare profanity, she crossed her legs, squirmed down in her seat, and made herself very still. She heard the bus driver's command to move, but she refused. And refused again. Next came the driver's radio call, and within minutes, a policeman entered the bus and arrested her.

Mary Louise was taken downtown, booked, and jailed. She was released two hours later, when her father arrived and paid the fourteen-

EMMETT TILL

What happened to Emmett Till in the summer of 1955 was a horrible reminder of how much resistance there would be to racial integration in the South. Till was a fourteen-year-old Negro boy from Chicago who had gone to Mississippi to visit relatives in a small town. In August 1955, he allegedly whistled at a white store clerk and said "Bye, baby" to her as he left the store. Three nights later he was kidnapped. Three days after that, his body was found floating in a river, wrapped in barbed wire and grotesquely mutilated. Two white men were arrested but acquitted by an all-white jury.

The savagery of the crime sent a chilling message. "We talked about it a lot that summer and in school the next fall," remembers Claudette. "There had been lynchings and cross burnings before, but this was a much stronger warning. Emmett Till was our age."

Emmett Till and his mother, Mamie Bradley

Mary Louise Smith,
graduation photo, 1955

dollar fine. It happened so quickly and quietly that there was no newspaper publicity. By the time E. D. Nixon and other black leaders heard about Mary Louise Smith, her fine had already been paid and it was too late to mount a legal challenge.

But that didn't stop people from talking. Another teenage girl had been arrested on the bus. Who was she? Where was she from? What church did her family go to? Who were her parents? Where did they live? Soon the rumor mill was spinning out gossip that the Smith girl's father was a drunk and the family lived in a squalid shack.

The truth was much different. Mary Louise later said she never in her life saw her father drunk. For one thing, he was too busy working to drink much. After Mary Louise's mother died, in 1952, Frank Smith took a second job to support his six children. Hardly a shack, the Smith home was a two-story, three-bedroom frame house in a working-class neighborhood. But Mary Louise Smith, the second teenager with the nerve to face down Jim Crow on a city bus, was, like Claudette, branded "unfit" to serve as the public face of a mass bus protest.

During the summer and fall of 1955, Montgomery's adult black activists thought hard about the buses—which looked increasingly like Jim Crow's Achilles' heel. Each considered what to do in his or her own way. Jo Ann Robinson, E. D. Nixon, Dr. Martin Luther King, Jr., and others continued to meet with city and bus officials, consistently pressing for black drivers, courteous treatment, and a revised seating plan. Every polite refusal increased their resolve. Dr. King thought the officials were digging their own grave. "The inaction of the city and bus officials after the

Colvin case would make it necessary for them . . . to meet another committee, infinitely more determined," he later wrote.

Rosa Parks and Fred Gray met for lunch nearly every day, often talking about what could be learned from Claudette's case that could end segregation on the buses. In July, Mrs. Parks slipped away for a two-week workshop on interracial relations at the Highlander Folk School in Tennessee. Here, for the first time, she saw blacks and whites treated as equals. She returned saying it had changed her life.

The time was ripe for change. There was a growing impatience with segregation. Claudette had crossed a line, proclaiming that at least one young Alabaman would not share her future with Jim Crow. Seven months later, Mary Louise Smith had joined her. Now, a year and a half after *Brown v. Board of Education*, a few brave young people were demanding a different future. Education may have been the way up, but transportation was the way out. If they were branded "uncontrollable" or "emotional" or even "profane," so be it. Claudette and now Mary Louise Smith had shown through their courage that at least some young people were ready to act.

Rosa Parks with E. D. Nixon (at left). At last the African-American community of Montgomery was united and ready for action

CHAPTER SEVEN

"Another Negro Woman Has Been Arrested"

Bringing the gifts that my ancestors gave,
I am the dream and the hope of the slave.
I rise
I rise
I rise.
—Maya Angelou, "Still I Rise"

O N December 2, 1955, tens of thousands of black Montgomery residents studied an unsigned leaflet bearing a brief typewritten message. It began: "Another Negro woman has been arrested and thrown in jail because she refused to get up out of her seat on the bus for a white person to sit down. It is the second time since the Claudette Colbert [*sic*] case that a Negro woman has been arrested for the same thing. This has to be stopped." It concluded:

> We are, therefore, asking every Negro to stay off the buses Monday in protest of the arrest and trial. Don't ride the buses to work, to town, to school or anywhere on Monday. You can afford to stay out of school for one day if you have no other way to go except by bus. You can also afford to stay out of town for one day. If you work, take a cab, or walk. But please, children and grown-ups, don't ride the bus at all on Monday. Please stay off the buses Monday.

The author was Jo Ann Robinson, who had been up all night with two student assistants at Alabama State, feverishly running the flyers off on the college's mimeograph machine and bundling them into packages. When they finished, she placed a phone call to activate a network of distributors already in place. Soon twenty or so allies were stationed at their posts throughout the city, craning their necks watching for Robinson's car to come into view so they could receive their bundles of flyers and start passing them out in schools, offices, factories, stores, restaurants, and beauty parlors. "Read it and pass it on!" the distributors instructed and sped off. Two of Robinson's most trusted lieutenants were Claudette's favorite teachers, Miss Nesbitt and Miss Lawrence. By nightfall most blacks in Montgomery knew what was up. Those who didn't know about the one-day bus boycott read about it in the next morning's *Montgomery Advertiser*, in a story leaked by E. D. Nixon to a trusted reporter.

The "other Negro woman" arrested was Rosa Parks. Just the afternoon before, Mrs. Parks had refused a driver's command to give up her seat to a white passenger on a crowded bus. Then, as had been the case with Claudette, the driver called the police, officers boarded, and one asked her, "Why don't you stand up?" She replied, "Why do you push us around?" He answered, "I don't know, but the law is the law and you are under arrest."

There the similarity to Claudette's arrest ended. Rather than being grabbed by the wrists and jerked up from her seat with belongings flying everywhere, Rosa Parks stood up. One officer took her shopping bag, the other picked up her purse, and they escorted her off the bus and into a patrol car. She sat in the backseat alone, her hands uncuffed, as they drove to police headquarters and then to city hall. After her fingerprints were taken and the paperwork completed, she was allowed to telephone her family.

Soon E. D. Nixon and two white activists, Clifford and Virginia Durr, hurried downtown, paid her bond, and took her home, where Fred Gray later met her and agreed to be her lawyer. The next Monday morning, Mrs. Parks was found guilty in a brief court hearing. She was released upon payment of a ten-dollar fine and four dollars in court costs. Gray told the judge to expect an appeal. When Mrs. Parks walked out of the dim courthouse and into the cool, bright morning, she was surprised to find several hundred cheering supporters waiting for her.

Claudette had lit the fuse to a powder keg of protest, but her rebellion had caught black Montgomery by surprise. Now, nine months later, Rosa Parks was embraced by a community ready for action. Claudette had given them the time to prepare. As Fred Gray later said, "I don't mean to take anything away from Mrs. Parks, but Claudette gave all of us the moral courage to do what we did."

Married and in her early forties, Rosa Parks was widely known as an activist through her work with the Montgomery NAACP. As a seamstress at a downtown department store, she repaired, altered, and steam-pressed clothing—work known and respected by both the black professional class and ordinary workers. She was light-skinned but not white. She may not have gone to the Dexter Avenue Baptist Church—she was a Methodist—but she would have been accepted in any congregation. She bridged classes.

What she wasn't may have been just as important to Montgomery's black leadership, the preachers and teachers and ASC women and E. D. Nixon. She wasn't a teenager. Hardly "feisty" or "emotional," as Claudette was rumored to be, Rosa Parks struck almost everyone she met as a contained, pleasant, committed, and levelheaded individual. She was safe.

And she wasn't pregnant. Neither was Claudette when she had been arrested and people started talking about her, but now she was, and she would have to deal with it.

• • •

CLAUDETTE: The first few months I hoped and prayed and pretended it wasn't true, but it was. I had so little information about sex. I wasn't sexually active at all. I had never gone very far with my boyfriend, and my parents had never talked to me about sex. I would hear other girls say, "Well, I didn't get pregnant my first time, or the second." It had only happened once with this man, and I was so uninformed that I wasn't even sure that what we had done could get me pregnant.

But it had, and I thought my mom was going to have a heart attack when I told her. We thought about an abortion, but it was illegal, and the

only woman we had heard of who did abortions was supposedly connected with the police department. Besides, my mother was convinced
God wouldn't forgive you for an abortion. My dad threatened to kill the
father—he was so much older than I was. Then my dad got worried that
the father's wife's family was going to accuse me of breaking up their mar-
riage and come after us. My parents insisted that I not tell anyone who the
father was. I wanted to tell, to explain what had happened to me so that
people would understand, but I gave in and kept quiet.

My mom just took over my life at that point. Usually I was stronger, but
right then I was easy to control. Of course I couldn't marry the father; I
didn't love him and he was already married. My boyfriend, Fred Harvey,
came to our house and asked to marry me, but my mother said he would
just be doing it out of pity. I wanted to say yes, but I backed down.

We decided I'd keep my pregnancy a secret as long as I could so I
wouldn't get kicked out of school. The rule at Booker T. Washington was
"If you're pregnant, you're out." Then, when Christmas break came, I
would tell the school I was sick and go to Birmingham and live with my
birth mother and have the baby there. After that I would leave the baby
with her for a while and come back to Montgomery and finish high school.
I would only have one semester left.

But I started showing too early. Late in the fall a few girls caught on.
They'd say, "I thought you had more sense." I didn't have any answer to
that. The teachers always had an eye out for pregnant girls—it was very
common. They knew the signs. So one day I got called down to the office. I went in to see the principal, Mr. Smiley. I said, "I know why I'm
here; you don't have to bother saying it," but he did anyway. And he added,
"Don't come back after Christmas break."

So we had to change strategies. Our new plan was for me to have the
baby in Birmingham and finish school there. I had never officially changed
my last name on my birth certificate to Colvin—it still said I was Claudette
Austin. So I could enroll as Claudette Austin and finish high school in
Birmingham.

One day a few weeks before Christmas, I was at home, trying to get
ready in my mind for all the changes to come—changes in my body, be-

coming a mother, not going to Booker T. Washington, moving away from my Montgomery family—when a neighbor girl walked over from across the street carrying a piece of paper. She handed it to me and said, "You gotta read this." The three of us—her, me, and Mom—stood out in the front yard reading it. It was the boycott leaflet: "Don't ride the bus on Monday." Right away I saw my name—misspelled: "Claudette Colbert." My first thought was, If they had just called me, I could have at least reminded them how to spell my name.

But it didn't say who the Negro woman was who got arrested. When I heard on the news that it was Rosa Parks, I had several feelings: I was glad an adult had finally stood up to the system, but I felt left out. I was thinking, Hey, I did that months ago and everybody dropped me. There was a time when I thought I would be the centerpiece of the bus case. I was eager to keep going in court. I had wanted them to keep appealing my case. I had enough self-confidence to keep going. Maybe adults thought a teenager's testimony wouldn't hold up in the legal system. But what I did know is they all turned their backs on me, especially after I got pregnant. It really, really hurt. But on the other hand, having been with Rosa at the NAACP meetings, I thought, Well, maybe she's the right person—she's strong and adults won't listen to me anyway. One thing was for sure: no matter how I felt or what I thought, I wasn't going to get my chance.

• • •

DR. MARTIN LUTHER KING, JR., rose early the morning of Monday, December 5, rushed to his picture window, and peered out at the first buses as they moved past his house. They were nearly empty. Usually they were filled with maids and black schoolchildren. Excited, he jumped in his car and drove around Montgomery to inspect other buses during the morning commute. In an hour of driving, he saw a total of only eight black passengers on the buses. Clearly the message "Please . . . don't ride the bus at all on Monday" had reached almost everyone.

That evening, a "mass meeting" was held at the Holt Street Baptist Church, to celebrate the day's triumph and to plan for the future. By 7:00 p.m., nearly one thousand people were wedged shoulder to shoulder inside the brightly lit church, while four thousand more gathered outside

The Reverend Martin Luther King, Jr., was a passionate speaker.
For Claudette, his speeches "just brought out everything
you wanted to say to a white person"

in the chilly darkness to hear songs and speeches and prayers broadcast through makeshift speakers.

Dr. King, elected just that morning as president of the Montgomery Improvement Association, was the main speaker. It was his first major public speech that wasn't a church sermon, and he needed to inspire this crowd. When introduced, he grasped the sides of the pulpit and took a moment to collect himself. Turning to Rosa Parks, seated behind him in a special place of honor, he began, "Just last Thursday . . . one of the finest citizens in Montgomery . . . was taken from a bus—and carried to jail and arrested—because she refused to give up—to give her seat to a white person . . . And since it had to happen, I'm happy it happened to a person like Mrs. Parks, for nobody can doubt the boundless outreach of her integrity. Nobody can doubt the height of her character, nobody can doubt the depth of her Christian commitment."

Toward the end of his address, Dr. King delivered lines for which he would be remembered. "And we are determined here in Montgomery," he said, his voice rising in intensity, "to work and fight until justice runs down like water and righteousness like a mighty stream." His passionate words rocked the church. "Standing beside love is always justice," he continued. "Not only are we using the tools of persuasion—but we've got to use the tools of coercion." When King sat down to thunderous applause, the crowd inside and outside was ready to act. The Reverend Ralph Abernathy took the pulpit and read a resolution asking that all citizens refrain from riding buses operated by Montgomery City Lines, Inc. "All in favor of the motion, stand," Abernathy said. Everyone in the room climbed to their feet.

It was the first of millions and millions of steps to come. The Montgomery bus boycott was born.

• • •

CLAUDETTE: Mom and Velma went to the mass meeting, but I stayed home. I was in a different mind. I was depressed, I was pregnant, I had been expelled from school, and I was leaving home. I had already taken the NAACP records back to Rosa's house and left them with her mother.

Right before Christmas, Mom drove Velma and me to Birmingham. We had Christmas there with my birth mother's family and visited some friends. Then Mom and Velma went back to Montgomery. I was on my own.

That was an important time for me. My parents were so strict, especially Mom. She tried to make all the decisions for me. Being away from her in Birmingham gave me a chance to clear my head. I thought a lot about what was going down in Montgomery.

MLK'S BOYHOOD BUS EXPERIENCE

Martin Luther King, Jr., knew firsthand about bitter times on the bus. When he was fourteen, he traveled from Atlanta to a Georgia town to take part in a speech contest. On the way home a white bus driver ordered King and his teacher to give up their seats to white riders. King refused at first, but his teacher persuaded him to give way. He had to stand for several hours. Twenty years later he called it "the angriest I have ever been in my life."

A protest of some kind had been coming on for a long time. Black people weren't going to take segregation much longer. If you were black, you experienced abuse every day of your life. Every day. You couldn't even walk through the park without looking over your shoulder for a policeman. The bus boycott was a way of expressing anger at the system at last.

I was thinking, Where are we going? In church the adults kept saying Reverend King would eventually be driven out of Montgomery or they'd murder him, since whites would never give in. People were saying the boycott wouldn't succeed. But I was glad it was happening. So many black people were just struggling from day to day—most of us. We had to do it. There had been so much injustice, from Jeremiah Reeves to all the horror stories involving black women abused by white men, to my own arrest. I really wanted to be a part of the boycott.

I also used the time to clear my head about my own life. When I left Montgomery, everyone was saying I was "mental" and "crazy." But I wasn't. The most horrifying part of my last year hadn't been finding out I was pregnant, or getting kicked out of school. It was the sound of the jailer's key in the cell door. It was my arrest. And I had gotten through that. The pregnancy was, in a way, a chance to regroup and think about my life. I was a healthy young woman and I was going to have this baby, and I would deal with motherhood when it came. I could take the G.E.D.— a high school equivalency exam—in Montgomery and get my diploma that way.

I only stayed in Birmingham about two weeks. I missed my dad, Q.P. He was always there for me. Besides, I'd had justice on my mind for a long time. Just because I was pregnant didn't change my mission. I had been talking about revolution ever since Jeremiah Reeves. I wanted to be part of the bus boycott even if I couldn't be a leader. I had helped get all this started.

So I went back home.

Members of Montgomery's black community gather at the
Holt Street Baptist Church in support of the boycott

CHAPTER EIGHT

SECOND FRONT, SECOND CHANCE

We are going to hold our stand. We are not going to be a part
of any program that will get Negroes to ride the buses again
at the price of the destruction of our heritage and way of life.
—W. A. "Tacky" Gayle, mayor of Montgomery

WITH THE TURN of the new year of 1956, Montgomery throbbed with excitement. Day by day, reporters and photographers poured into town to cover the Negro bus protest in the heart of Dixie. As the boycott entered its second month, black leaders continued to press for the same three modest changes that Jo Ann Robinson and others had requested two years earlier—which did not include integrated seating—but city officials wouldn't budge. "Give them an inch and they'll take a mile," they told one another. The City Lines bus company declared the proposed changes illegal and said that, unfortunately, their hands were tied.

Mass meetings continued at black churches every Tuesday and Thursday night. Young, round-faced Dr. Martin Luther King, Jr., who urged boycotters to refrain from violence and seek charity toward whites in their hearts, inspired crowds with stirring speeches that often included ideas and philosophies from distant times and places. He talked about the power of love to change the world. "He had poetry in his voice, and he could snatch scripture outa the air and make it hum," said E. D. Nixon, who admitted "he was saying it better 'n I ever could." King began to emerge as a charismatic national figure.

Determined to apply economic pressure peacefully, black protesters let

THE MONTGOMERY IMPROVEMENT ASSOCIATION

Leaders believed that a new organization was needed to run the boycott, so they created the Montgomery Improvement Association (MIA). Determined to avoid friction between established black leaders, they nominated as president a newcomer, Dr. Martin Luther King, Jr., pastor of the Dexter Avenue Baptist Church. "Well, if you think I can render some service, I will," he replied. A board of twenty-five directors was named.

After thousands voted to continue the boycott beyond one day, the MIA had a lot of work to do. They had to design the car pool, put it in motion, and pay for it. Mass meetings were held twice a week to keep spirits up and collect donations. As the boycott rolled on, donations poured in from all over the country—eventually enough for the MIA to buy more than thirty station wagons.

Some teens organized their social lives around the mass meetings. Annie Larkin, then sixteen, recalls, "I'd go home from school, get my homework done, and my grandmother would have dinner ready so my aunt and I could go to mass meetings together. I went every Tuesday and Thursday night, no matter where."

the nearly empty buses rumble on by like green ghosts, ignoring the doors that snapped open invitingly at the corners, and devised their own transportation system. Coached by leaders of Baton Rouge's bus boycott of 1953, the Montgomery Improvement Association (MIA) designed an alternative to the buses on the scale of a wartime military transport system, moving tens of thousands of maids and yard men and clerks and students around Montgomery's far-flung neighborhoods every day. And it was entirely voluntary—it ran on dedication, generosity, and hope.

The MIA network was unveiled in detail at a mass meeting on December 12. There would be forty-two morning pickup "stations" and forty-eight evening stations scattered throughout Montgomery. These points had been carefully plotted on maps by mail carriers, the workers who knew the city best. The central dispatch station would be a black-owned downtown parking lot, manned by an on-call transportation committee. The "buses" would be a giant car pool consisting of ordinary people's automobiles. Car owners were asked to lend their vehicles to the MIA car pool so that other people could drive them around town. For most people, especially if they had little money, having a car was a proud symbol of status. Letting total strangers drive one's car around all day was a hard thing to ask, but nearly two hundred people turned over their keys to the boycott.

Here's how it worked: a maid needing to get across town to her white employer's home would walk to the morning station nearest her home and wait for a ride. After work she would walk to the nearest night station to be picked up and driven to a drop-off point nearer her home. Since it was against the law for private cars to charge fares like licensed taxis, the network would be paid for by donations collected at the mass meetings. Most of the rides would be free.

Though the network was elegantly designed, there were not enough seats in the car pool to replace an entire city bus system. Thousands of black workers, including many who were elderly and some who were disabled, set out from home in the predawn darkness and walked miles each

The third month of the boycott and another day of walking

Boycott supporters climb out of one of the dozens of station wagons that were purchased during the 381-day protest. Many of the vehicles were assigned to churches

day. Some preferred to walk to show their support for the boycott rather than accept a ride even from the MIA car pool. One MIA driver told the story of having come upon an elderly woman hobbling along the road. "Jump in, grandmother," he said to her, pushing open the door. She waved him on. "I'm not walking for myself," she said. "I'm walking for my children and my grandchildren."

Family members made enormous sacrifices and sometimes hobbled home with barely enough energy to eat supper. And family chores like shopping had to continue. That meant more steps. The foot-weary warriors told their stories at the mass meetings, inspiring and encouraging one another to keep walking.

Many were initially skeptical of the boycott. "When they first sent the leaflets saying 'don't ride the bus,' I was worried about my momma," remembers Alean Bowser. "I got angry, and I said they'd better not do anything to her. I thought she'd still go on riding the bus because she did housecleaning and she worked far away from home. But then they had worked out this whole plan of having people to drive and pick up. I got behind it. I and three other girls from my typing class at school started working at the Baptist Center, typing up and mimeographing lists of the people who were driving in the bus boycott. We had to make the list every third night in order to keep the information current. They had stations downtown. Who was driving this direction and that direction. I had to call the drivers and make sure they were still willing and available. And people in most families had walking jobs, too. I was appointed to walk downtown and pay our bills. But I could use the network for that, too."

• • •

CLAUDETTE: When I got back to Montgomery, of course I stayed off the buses. Mostly I rode with my mom in a used Plymouth Dad bought for her. She needed it, because she worked way up out of town in a place the car pool didn't go to.

Dad was very frugal. He saved enough to buy a TV set, too, so we could keep up with the boycott. We'd watch the news every night. The boycott was always the headline—it was the biggest story in the South. I also read Jo Ann Robinson's editorials in a little newsletter that came every month.

The people Mom worked for were sympathetic to the boycott. The

Q. P. Colvin, Claudette's dad, bought a car for the family during the boycott

77

WHITE SUPPORT OF THE BOYCOTT

Not all white Montgomerians opposed the boycott, and not all favored racial segregation. A small but determined minority of white citizens assisted the car pool, drove their black employees to and from work, and sometimes donated money to the boycott. Among the best known were Robert Graetz, the pastor of Trinity Lutheran Church, and Clifford Durr, a lawyer who assisted Fred Gray in his legal cases. His wife, Virginia Durr, also provided support in many ways.

A few whites dared to express their support publicly. Juliette Morgan, a librarian, wrote in a letter to the editor of the *Montgomery Advertiser*, "It is hard . . . not to be moved with admiration at the quiet dignity, discipline, and dedication with which the Negroes have conducted their boycott."

The death threats began immediately, by phone and mail. They increased month by month. People hurled stones at Morgan's picture window and sprinted up to ring her doorbell again and again in the dead of night, shattering her sleep. She lost many friends. About a year after her letter was published, Juliette Morgan took her own life.

first sign of this was they didn't fire Mom when they found out I was arrested. They weren't rich; they were just average people. They paid my mom three dollars a day and bus fare. The lady used to bring her home after work on the days when Mom didn't drive.

The boycott was relatively easy for people on King Hill because we already had our own community transportation system in place. We were isolated—just three little streets on top of a hill on the edge of town. We had no stores up there, so we had to go through white neighborhoods to shop downtown. To get off the Hill, three or four people would pitch in to pay someone a quarter to drive them to and from work. They'd drop the maids off house by house because everybody was going in the same direction.

My family duties increased during the boycott. Mom was gone a lot, because she used her car to drive people places. We didn't donate our Plymouth to the boycott because Mom needed it to get out of town for work, but since we had a car people were constantly coming around to say, "Mary

Ann, can you take me and a couple of others to this place or that?" Dad didn't drive and I didn't have a license yet, so I did more cooking and cleaning and shopping and laundry while Mom drove. I had several cousins who drove taxis, and they'd come and take me to town when I wanted. A lot of people volunteered their cars for the boycott and dipped into their savings to buy gasoline during that time. Everyone pulled together.

I went to the mass meetings when they were at churches on the other side of town, where people wouldn't recognize me. I went to a lot of them, more than once a month. I heard Dr. King speak, and felt the people rally around him. Those speeches he made just brought out everything you wanted to say to a white person. People were kicking you when you were down every day, and his words made you feel stronger. I sat in the back, far away from the speechmakers, wearing big shirts to cover my growing stomach. The leaders sure weren't going to invite a pregnant teenager up on-stage during a mass meeting. It bothered me to be shunned, but I was an unwed pregnant girl and I knew how people were. People who recognized me would ask, "Who's the father?" I'd answer, "None of your business."

• • •

BY LATE JANUARY, the City Lines bus company was losing $3,200 a day. They had been forced to lay off drivers and shut down several bus routes just to stay in business. Inspired at mass meetings by the testimony of elderly people who walked great distances and poor families who donated money for gasoline, protesters kept walking and vowed to do so until justice came. Many who owned cars continued to offer them to the car pool and volunteer as drivers. Thousands used the car pool each day, and thousands more walked to work and school and the downtown stores.

In desperation, Mayor W. A. "Tacky" Gayle turned up the heat. Police were instructed to crack down on drivers, stopping them and questioning them at every opportunity. Dr. King was arrested on January 26 for going thirty miles per hour in a twenty-five-mile-an-hour zone. He spent a night in jail for the first time in his life. Three days later someone hurled a bomb through his front window, causing extensive damage but injuring no one in his family. At a mass meeting he said, "If I am stopped, this movement will not stop, because God is with this movement."

Montgomery motorcycle police keep a close eye on a downtown parking lot, one of the many busy transfer points for the MIA car pool

The attacks continued. In early February a stick of dynamite landed on E. D. Nixon's front lawn. About that time Jo Ann Robinson's picture window was shattered by a huge rock, which her neighbors said had been thrown by a policeman. Days later two men dressed in full police uniform walked into the carport beside Robinson's house and scattered acid over her Chrysler sedan. According to neighbors, when they were finished, the pair calmly walked to their squad car and drove away. The substance burned holes the size of silver dollars through the vehicle's top, fenders, and hood. Neighbors told Robinson what they saw but were too frightened to make an official report of the crime.

With violence mounting and negotiations stalled, protesters asked one another how this would end. While everyone longed and prayed for success, many held private doubts—it was hard to imagine that whites would ever give up control.

Fred Gray thought he saw the way out—it was the same path he had envisioned from the day he heard of Claudette's arrest. Why not go to court and sue the city of Montgomery and the state of Alabama, arguing that if segregated schools were unconstitutional—as the U.S. Supreme Court had ruled in *Brown v. Board of Education*—then weren't segregated buses? Instead of politely asking for modest reforms in seating patterns and more courteous behavior from the drivers, why not try to obliterate the segregation laws in court? If judges agreed, the city would have to give up. Once the buses were integrated, there would be no *need* for a bus boycott.

Gray, like the NAACP lawyers in New York who were closely following the boycott, was tired of playing defense. He wanted to mount a legal attack on behalf of all black riders as a class-action suit, not just to defend protesters who got arrested and charged as criminals one by one. Success would depend on putting the right case in front of the right judges in the right courtroom.

Since judges representing the state of Alabama and the city of Montgomery court systems were all but certain to be hostile, the lawyers knew that their only chance was to argue their case in a federal court, where judges might listen with an open mind to an antisegregation suit offered by black lawyers.

Any lawsuit challenging the constitutionality of a state law was supposed to be heard by a panel of three judges in a federal court—that was the rule. Whether federal judges based in Alabama would actually follow it and hear the case was the big question. If they did, the suit would still be heard and decided in Alabama, but the judges would represent the *United States* government, not the state of Alabama or the city of Montgomery.

The Montgomery Improvement Association voted to let Gray go

SEPARATE BUT EQUAL?

In 1896, in a famous court case known as *Plessy v. Ferguson*, the U.S. Supreme Court ruled that the state of Louisiana could racially segregate its buses, streetcars, and trains without violating the U.S. Constitution as long as the separate sections of compartments were "equal."

Separate but equal became the legal basis for segregation throughout the South. But the idea that the schools, parks, hotels, restaurants, and sections of buses and trains were "equal" was a sham. In 1900, $15.41 was spent on each white child in the public schools versus $1.50 per black student. The ratio was the same forty years later.

It was this idea—separate but equal—that the Supreme Court justices struck down in *Brown v. Board of Education of Topeka* in 1954. The justices wrote, "We conclude, unanimously, that in the field of public education the doctrine of 'separate but equal' has no place." But did it still have a place in transportation? Sixty years after *Plessy v. Ferguson*, Fred Gray and the other lawyers were fashioning a lawsuit to insist that the answer was no.

ahead with the lawsuit—the "second front," as it came to be called—and raise money to pay for it. Gray went to New York to huddle over legal strategies with NAACP lawyers, then returned to Montgomery and filed the suit in the federal building. To his delight, the suit was accepted as a constitutional challenge to state law and assigned to a three-judge federal panel.

Next Gray began to look for plaintiffs—those people whose names would appear on the lawsuit and who would testify in court. The idea was to put on the witness stand black passengers who would testify to how Jim Crow had made their lives miserable while they were just trying to get from place to place.

Courage would be their number one requirement. They would be placing their lives in grave danger, and the lives of those they lived with. From their seat in a tiny witness box in a packed courtroom, plaintiffs would face aggressive white lawyers firing questions at them as white judges looked on. Fred Gray knew well that all their lives black people had been taught to defer to whites. Somehow these plaintiffs would have to find the steel to speak freely and the composure to think clearly while seated in a pressure chamber. And they would need to have a good story to tell.

The lawyers ruled out Rosa Parks. Her case was still being appealed, and they wanted the new federal lawsuit to be independent of any existing criminal case. The MIA members proposed many candidates, and Gray interviewed the most promising. In the end, he whittled the list down to five names. All were women. This was because more women than men rode the buses, and because Gray and his colleagues wanted to protect the jobs of men, who were typically regarded as the breadwinners in families. All five women Gray selected had been bullied and insulted and cheated on buses, and all were still angry about it. It may have been a short list, but Gray thought it was a good one.

Ironically, the only one of the five who had previously appeared in court on a bus case was the youngest. But she had gone through the most. She had been tested by fire. Claudette Colvin had been on Fred Gray's short list from the moment he conceived the suit. He picked up the phone and dialed a familiar King Hill number.

• • •

CLAUDETTE: When Fred Gray called our house in January, we were all surprised. The boycott was almost two months old, and I hadn't heard from any of the leaders since it started, not even Rosa Parks. I was seven months pregnant. But we told him to come on out.

He arrived one evening with his secretary, Bernice. We sat around the coffee table in our living room, just as we had the year before, after I got arrested. He was still dressed in a dark suit and he still talked like a lawyer. Bernice still took dictation. The only change was my big belly. He described the case and discussed what would be expected of me if I took part. Because I was still a minor, he asked my parents if they would let me do it. Mom and Dad said yes.

Then he asked me. I was sitting on the piano stool. Bernice's fingers moved whenever I spoke. He didn't mention that there would be anyone else in the suit. I thought I was going to appear alone. As I listened, I was of two minds. In one mind I was afraid. The way life was in the South, how could you not be afraid? You never knew who was KKK, or who

83

would target you. Every day on the radio, I'd hear angry white callers shouting that the Communists had invaded the black churches and people had to act now.

But I was not a person who lived in fear. My mom had always said, "If God is for you, the Devil can't do you any harm," and that's how I felt, too. We all just lived that way. And I felt that if they really needed someone, I was the right person. It was a chance for me to speak out. I was still angry. I wanted white people to know that I wasn't satisfied with segregation. Black people, too. And it didn't sound like the trial would happen until after my baby was born. You had to do what you had to do. So I said yes.

• • •

"WE TALKED TO ALL THE FAMILY AT ONCE," remembers Fred Gray, "and there was no reservation on anyone's part. I wouldn't have taken anyone with any reservation. I told them what would happen, what they would be subjected to. That there would be phone calls, there would be threats. I liked that family. They were self-sufficient. If there had been reprisals, they would have still gotten by. It took real courage to be a plaintiff in that suit. It wasn't easy. And Claudette was the youngest."

• • •

CLAUDETTE: After they left, my mom called our pastor, Reverend Johnson, and told him what Fred Gray had asked me to do. And my reverend came out to my home. Some of my neighbors were already afraid to talk to me. White Citizens Councils had formed to take jobs away from people who joined the boycott. I felt like no one wanted to be near me because I was so outspoken about ending segregation.

But Reverend Johnson really knew me and cared for me and stood by me. He worried about how I was going to hold up against those white people drilling me in court. He knew the terror was real. He knew what the stakes were. At my home he took my hands very gently and said to me, "Claudette, do you really feel up to it?" And once again I heard myself say, "Yes, Reverend Johnson, I do."

My baby was born in Montgomery on March 29, 1956. I named him Raymond, after my uncle. Velma was with me in the hospital. Raymond came out very fair-skinned with blond hair and blue eyes. At the hospital, the attendants kept bringing him in and asking me the name of his father. I wouldn't tell them. They didn't believe the father was black, and they held it against me. I would cover my head up because I didn't want to hear the awful things they were saying about us. I didn't need to hear that. I loved Raymond from the moment I saw him.

Claudette's pastor, Rev. H. H. Johnson, makes a point at a mass meeting. Rev. Martin Luther King, Jr. (left) and E. D. Nixon stand beside him

I only had about six weeks after Raymond's birth to get ready for the boycott lawsuit. I wanted to get my body ready so I could fit into a good dress, and to get my mind ready, too. I rehearsed what I wanted to say. I prayed. My mother had always said, "If you can even talk to a white person without lowering your eyes you're really doing something." Well, I was determined to do that and more. Miss Nesbitt said, "Claudette, you always wanted to be in plays, to do Shakespeare. Now here is your stage." And she was right: I had been speaking out against injustice since ninth grade.

At night, while I would lie in bed and rehearse the things I was going to say, Raymond slept beside me in a little bassinet. It was just the two of us in the front room, him breathing or fussing or pulling at his bottle, and me thinking about what I would say at the trial. Sometimes I thought about Harriet Tubman, about her courage. I prayed I could have her kind of courage on the trial day.

Or sometimes I would imagine, Claudette, you're a Christian, and you're about to get thrown to the lions and you have one speech to give to the Senate.

That was more like it. In my imagination that courtroom seemed like the Colosseum, and it felt like I had one last speech. I was going to make the most of it.

PART TWO

PLAYING FOR KEEPS

Browder versus Gayle *changed relationships of blacks
and whites in America and the world.
Yet few people know about the case and even fewer
know about the plaintiffs.*
—Filmmaker and journalist William Dickerson-Waheed,
Rivers of Change

*All the boycotts and sit-ins and marches in themselves
did not cure the illness of discrimination.
It was the court decisions that did it.*
—Judge Frank M. Johnson, Jr.

Advertiser

Complete CAPITAL EDITION

February 2, 1956   36 Pages ★   Price 5 Cents

TRAVEL BARRIER CHALLENGED

5 Negroes Attack Segregation Laws In Federal Court

By JOE AZBELL
Advertiser City Editor

Five Montgomery Negro women yesterday filed a suit in the U.S. District Court asking that the courts declare Alabama and Montgomery transportation segregation laws unconstitutional.

The suit, entered in the court at 12:45 p.m. by Attys. Fred Gray and Charles Langford, was filed by Aureha S. Browder, Susie McDonald, Jeanette Reese, Claudette Colvin by Q. P. Colvin, her father, and Mary Louise Smith by Frank Smith, her father.

Named as defendants were Mayor W. A. Gayle, Commissioner Clyde Sellers, Commissioner Frank Parks, individually and as the City Commission, Police Chief G. J. Ruppenthal, the Montgomery City Lines and bus drivers James F. Blake and Robert Cleere.

BULKY DOCUMENT

The bulky court document specifically asks:

1. A final judgment and decree that will declare and define the legal rights of the parties in the controversy.

2. A final judgment and decree that will declare Section 301, Title 48, Code of Alabama and Sections 10 and 11 of the Montgomery City Code, (ordering bus segregation), null and void.

3. A judgment and decree declaring that the acts of the defendants in seeking to compel the

ONLY DAMAGE TO FENCE

Officials Probing Blast In NAACP Leader's Yard

By STEVE LESHER

An explosive was tossed on the 647 Clinton Ave. last night. No one was injured.

It was the second bombing this week of property owned by Negroes prominent in the boycott of the Montgomery City Lines by Negroes.

Nixon is former state president of the NAACP and current president of the Montgomery Progressive Democratic Assn.

No damage was done to the violating the state segregation laws by refusing to yield her seat on a bus to a white person.

The first bombing occurred at King's home at about 10 p.m. on Monday. King was not at home at the time but the house was occupied by his wife, his daughter and a friend. The explosive, which Toxicologist Pruitt said was "one stick of dynamite or a hand grenade," landed on the porch of King's home and broke out several windows, split a prch

---

s a nation-
rument of-
opportunity
ephoto

de
AY
ON

The *Montgomery Advertiser*, February 2, 1956, front page news

CHAPTER NINE

BROWDER V. GAYLE

Our whole strategy is based on the May 11 trial.
—Dr. Martin Luther King, Jr.

May 11, 1956

CLAUDETTE: I woke up to the smell of coffee like any other day. Every day no matter what, Mom'd get up and make biscuits, grits, and sausage, bacon, eggs, or ham. I bottle-fed Raymond. Then Mama Sweetie came over with her daughter, Scrap, to take care of Raymond while Q.P. and I went to the trial. Mom had to work. Mama Sweetie was still a big part of my life. She had moved from Pine Level to Montgomery a few years after we had. She was about seventy now, a little more wrinkled but still petite and still kind. Just the sound of her voice in the house made me think things would be all right.

It was cool out but not rainy. I was glad I didn't have to wear a rain bonnet. I pumped milk from my breasts so that I wouldn't leak and put on my best dress, light blue with a cummerbund and a V cut. It looked good on me in the mirror. I drank my coffee slowly and thought about the day to come.

Then my cousin James Henderson pulled up to drive us to the courthouse. Before we left, we all bowed our heads and Mom said a prayer. We were around the table—me, Mom, Q.P. in his chair, Mama Sweetie, Scrap, James, and little Raymond in his bassinet. Mom prayed for me to have courage, and for Fred Gray to do his best, and for success in defeating this horrible system. Then we all said the Lord's Prayer and we went on our way.

By the time we pulled up to the courthouse, there was already a big crowd waiting outside: men in suits and brimmed hats, and women wearing their best Sunday dresses. There were cameramen out on the sidewalk. I got out and went looking for Fred Gray.

• • •

THE CROWD HAD ASSEMBLED EARLY outside the federal courthouse because May 11, 1956, was a big day. It was the 159th day of the Montgomery bus boycott, with no end in sight. The lawsuit meant hope. Some boycotters had been stationed on the courthouse steps since dawn. One black laborer explained his presence to a reporter from *Jet* magazine by saying he had already walked 335 miles to and from work since the boycott started. But, he said, "while they're juggling that hot potato [the lawsuit] I'll keep on footin' it."

Legs were tired and nerves frayed. Cash to keep the car pool going was hard to raise. Negotiations between black leaders and white authorities had

THE FOURTEENTH AMENDMENT TO THE U.S. CONSTITUTION

In *Browder v. Gayle*, lawyers representing black riders claimed that the segregation laws governing Montgomery's city buses violated the Fourteenth Amendment to the U.S. Constitution. Ratified in 1868 to secure freedom for slaves, the Fourteenth Amendment said in section one,

No State shall make or enforce any law which shall abridge the privileges or immunities of citizens of the United States; nor shall any State deprive any person of life, liberty, or property, without due process of law; nor deny to any person within its jurisdiction the equal protection of the laws.

This amendment was used in several important cases during the civil rights era to dismantle legal segregation, including *Brown v. Board of Education of Topeka*.

One hundred boycott leaders were indicted on conspiracy charges. All pleaded not guilty, including (top row) Fred Gray and Jo Ann Robinson; (bottom row) Rosa Parks, Rev. Martin Luther King, Jr., and E. D. Nixon

hardened into a tense stalemate, with the whole Southern way of life at stake. Just a few weeks before, Mayor Gayle and the entire Montgomery City Council had made a public show of joining the White Citizens Council in a packed coliseum with thousands cheering their approval. The council was a group of powerful politicians and businesspeople dedicated to keeping Montgomery segregated.

Segregationists singled out Reverend Martin Luther King, Jr., branding him a "troublemaker," an "outsider" who had come from Atlanta to stir up local blacks. They bombed his house and threatened his life by mail and telephone. He remained outwardly unflappable. According to one magazine account, when someone called in the middle of the night to threaten "that N—— who's running the bus boycott," his wife calmly answered, "My husband is asleep . . . He told me to write the name and number of anyone who called to threaten his life so that he could return the call and receive the threat in the morning when he wakes up and is fresh."

City leaders convinced themselves that blacks really wanted to ride the buses but that King's silver tongue had seduced them into rebellion. Police harassed boycotters as they waited at pickup stations for their MIA cars, ordering them to move on, threatening to charge them with loitering or hitchhiking—both crimes.

On February 21 a grand jury had indicted—formally accused of a crime—100 blacks for violating an obscure 1921 law banning boycotts "without just or legal cause." Those charged included Dr. King, twenty-three other ministers, and all the car-pool drivers. Rosa Parks was indicted, as were Jo Ann Robinson, E. D. Nixon, and Fred Gray. Claudette was not named, though her minister, the Reverend H. H. Johnson, was. The boycotters decided not to wait for the sheriff to come and arrest them. E. D. Nixon strode right into the county courthouse, saying, "Are you looking for me? Well here I am." He was booked, fingerprinted, photographed, and released on bond, wearing a broad smile as he stepped out of the courthouse. This touched off a parade of boycott leaders who filed inside the courthouse one by one and minutes later came out, freshly booked and fingerprinted, descending the steps into a cheering crowd of spectators. Fred Gray, one of those arrested, later recalled that it had been an honor to have been arrested, and that those not indicted felt a little insulted.

But it was this "hot potato," this lawsuit *Browder v. Gayle* (named after the plaintiff, Aurelia Browder, whose last name came first alphabetically, and W. A. "Tacky" Gayle, the mayor of Montgomery), that offered the first and best chance for blacks to end the boycott with a clean victory. This time it was *their* lawsuit, not one brought against them. This time *they* were using the Constitution, the rule book for *their* country, to achieve justice.

The crowd of dark-skinned figures in neatly pressed suits and church dresses had set off for the block-long federal courthouse just after dawn because *Browder v. Gayle* offered hope. Standing outside the courthouse that morning, E. D. Nixon looked around the crowd of his neighbors and friends and felt proud. "You could read a happiness on their faces, like they knew already that they were about to see the start of something very special," he later recalled. "There was a feeling of comfort going into the federal courthouse, which was very different from going [to the] county courthouse . . . We felt like we was protected here."

It had been exactly one hundred days since Fred Gray had filed papers to start this lawsuit, and they had been one hundred hard days of walking and doing without and praying. But May 11, 1956, the day of the trial, was finally here, and it was a sparkling spring morning. It was their day in court at last.

The courthouse doors opened, and spectators formed a line behind the security checkpoint. They took elevators to the second floor—blacks in one elevator, whites in another—and stepped into a large, dark, wood-paneled courtroom with a spacious, high ceiling. Tall windows were

JUDGE FRANK M. JOHNSON, JR.

The judge who sat just to the right of the witness stand was the youngest and most recently appointed of the three federal judges in the courtroom. In fact, *Browder v. Gayle* was the first big case for thirty-seven-year-old Frank M. Johnson, who had just been appointed by President Eisenhower as the new federal judge for the middle district of Alabama.

Johnson later became famous for presiding over landmark cases of the civil rights era, including the decision to let activists march from Selma to Montgomery, Alabama, without police interference. He also ruled that blacks could sit on Alabama juries and that Alabama's schools must be desegregated. He made it much easier for blacks to vote and required that black state troopers be hired in numbers equal to whites.

At first, observers assumed Judge Johnson would reliably rule with segregationists, since he was from Alabama. But nobody could predict what Frank Johnson would do. He ruled according to the merits of the case. His independence came naturally: Johnson had grown up in Winston County, a small pocket of northern Alabama that had sided with the North during the Civil War. His great-grandfather had fought for Lincoln and the Union.

framed by pale yellow drapes, pulled back now so that sunshine flooded the chamber, throwing soft spotlights onto the blue carpet. Behind the three empty judges' chairs, a great round-faced clock with Roman numerals was embedded into the wall. To the left of the clock stood the flag of the United States, with all forty-eight stars brilliant against a navy field. On the opposite side was the Alabama flag, sporting red bars crossed diagonally against a white field, fixed in the same pattern as the stars and bars of the Confederate flag.

About one hundred spectators, mostly blacks, settled into seats behind a rail on the main floor, and about one hundred more took the stairs to seats in a balcony above. Media were banned from the courtroom, but dozens of reporters and photographers staked out positions in front of the courthouse. Dr. King and Jo Ann Robinson were among the boycott leaders in attendance. As the hands on the big clock closed in on nine o'clock, the air buzzed with expectancy, like the tension before a prizefight.

The crowd's murmur subsided when the plaintiff team, including Fred Gray, several other lawyers, Claudette, and the other three black women, entered the courtroom and took their seats on the right side of a central aisle. There were only four plaintiffs now, since one of the women, Jeanette Reese, had dropped out under pressure from her employer. The city's attorneys and key witnesses took their seats on the left.

At one minute after 9:00, the bailiff bustled into the courtroom hollering, "All rise," followed close behind by three white men draped in black robes. Federal Justices Richard Rives, Seybourn Lynne, and Frank Johnson settled into adjacent thronelike chairs and stacked their papers on the polished bench before them. The crowd sat back down and listened as Justice Rives read out the plaintiffs' complaint, namely that laws and ordinances requiring segregated seating on public buses violated the equal rights provision of the Fourteenth Amendment of the U.S. Constitution. Justice Rives then turned to Fred Gray and said, "Call your first witness."

Gray had carefully planned the order in which he would present his four witnesses. He wanted to start fast, maintain a steady pace, and finish strong. He led off with Aurelia Browder, a sturdy, well-spoken, and confident thirty-seven-year-old ASC graduate with a strong history of involvement in community affairs. She had raised six children by herself as a seamstress after her husband's death. She had seen a lot of life and wasn't easily intimidated. Mrs. Browder was called to the witness stand, raised her right hand, and swore to tell the "truth, the whole truth, and nothing but the truth." She sat down.

Led by Gray's questioning, Mrs. Browder described herself as a long-time Montgomery resident who had ridden the bus "two or three times a day" until December 5, 1955. Why did she stop? "I knew if I would co-operate with my color [by boycotting] I would get [better treatment]," she explained. Gray asked if she had had "difficulty . . . in connection with the seating arrangements." She told of having been made to stand up by a bus driver so that whites could sit down. Gray asked, "If you were permitted to sit any place you wanted on the bus, would you be willing to ride it again?" She replied, "Yes, I would."

Gray then yielded the right to question Mrs. Browder to the city attorney Walter Knabe, who tried to induce her to say that the bus boycotters were nothing but puppets of Dr. Martin Luther King, Jr. Mrs. Browder would have none of it. After several futile questions, Knabe excused Mrs. Browder, and she returned to her seat.

The next two witnesses, Susie McDonald, seventy-seven, and Mary Louise Smith, who had by then turned nineteen, gave similar testimony to similar questions. McDonald, a widow and housekeeper for her son, said she was "often mistreated" on the bus and quit riding to support the boy-cott. She, too, said she would ride again if the buses were integrated and denied that she was under the spell of Dr. King. "I reached my own judg-ment," she said. "I stopped because I thought it was right and because we were mistreated."

Mary Louise Smith told of her refusal to get up from her bus seat for the red-haired white woman, and of the policeman's arrival. "I told him [the police officer], 'I am not going to move out of my seat. I got the priv-ilege to sit here like anybody else does.' " She also testified, "I would ride the city buses again provided we had no segregation on the city buses." Knabe tried to trap her into saying Dr. King had bewitched them all. "He [King] didn't represent no one," Mary Louise said. "We represented ourselves. We appointed him as our leader . . . he and his assistants." After Knabe yielded, she answered one question from Fred Gray and was dismissed.

Through Knabe's questioning of the first three witnesses, the city's strategy became clear. It had two parts:

1. To try to get witnesses to say that the black community had not objected to segregated bus seating before the boycott. Knabe reminded them that before, leaders had always pushed for black drivers, courteous treatment, and a different segregated seating plan—but never for an end to segregated seating. This was true, but only because leaders had never dared to hope for integrated seating until the U.S. Supreme Court had ruled against segregated schools, just two years before.

2. To show that Dr. King had stirred up all the trouble. The city tried to paint him as a silver-tongued outsider who never rode the bus in Montgomery himself but knew just how to make everyone who did feel unhappy. If it hadn't been for King, the city contended, blacks would be satisfied with things as they had always been.

As her turn to testify approached, Claudette fought the ever-tightening knot in her stomach. Fred Gray had deliberately saved her for last, for her story was the most powerful. She had been arrested, dragged from a bus, charged with breaking the segregation law, and jailed. She alone had fought the charges in court. She may have been only sixteen, but Claudette had more experience than anyone else when it came to challenging Jim Crow on the Montgomery buses. Proclaiming her constitutional rights as the police seized her wrists that day, she had objected not just to the seating plan on the bus but to the overall injustice of segregation. She had taken her stand without ever having spoken with Dr. King. Fred Gray and the other lawyers had faith in her. Mary Louise Smith stepped down from the witness stand, glancing at Claudette on the way back to her seat.

"Call your next witness, Mr. Gray," said Judge Rives.

"I call Claudette Colvin," said Fred Gray.

• • •

After Claudette raised her right hand and was sworn in, Fred Gray took a moment to go over his questions. From the witness box, Claudette felt hundreds of eyes settle upon her. She scanned the crowd for familiar faces. There was Jack Salter, a neighbor who worked at the federal courthouse. He gave her a thumbs-up from the back. She spotted A. C. James, her across-the-street neighbor who had come to lend support. And of course there was her dad, Q.P., smiling at her, always on her side and always there no matter what.

Fred Gray asked her to state her name and address and tell when she had stopped riding the buses. After that he led her through the account of her resistance and arrest on March 2, 1955. As Claudette related the

During *Browder v. Gayle*, Fred Gray points out the seating plan for city buses

story of her arrest, her voice became low, soft, and intense. Spectators leaned forward to hear her. The room gathered around the sound of her voice. When she described the policeman looming over her seat, she admitted that "I was very hurt . . . and I was crying . . . and the policeman said, 'I will have to take you off.' I didn't move at all . . . so he kicked me."

Claudette told of having been put into a car, handcuffed through the window, taken to city hall, and locked in an adult jail cell. At this point a spectator in the courtroom's balcony let out a wail and began sobbing loudly. Unable to stop crying, she finally stood and slowly made her way out of the courtroom.

Gray paused awhile, then looked up from his notes and said to Claudette, "Thank you . . . That's all."

But that wasn't all. Now came the hard part. Claudette kept her eyes trained on the city attorney Walter Knabe, a slender man with close-cut, sandy hair. Knabe tapped his pencil on his desk, glanced at his notes one last time, and then advanced toward her, his eyes fixed on hers. The three judges listened intently.

Knabe began: "You and the other Negroes have changed your ideas since December fifth, have you not?"

Claudette shook her head. "No, sir. We haven't changed our ideas. It has been in me ever since I was born."

Knabe persisted. "But the group stopped riding the buses for certain named things . . . that is correct, isn't it? . . . for certain things that Reverend King said were the things they objected to."

"No, sir," Claudette answered. "It was in the beginning when they arrested me, when they seen how dirty they treated the Negro girls here, that they had begun to feel like that . . . although some of us just didn't have the guts to stand up."

"Did you have a leader?" Knabe asked.

"Did we have a leader? Our leaders is just we, ourselves."

"But *somebody* spoke for the group."

"We all spoke for ourselves."

Knabe kept hammering at the point he was trying to get Claudette to make for him. "Did you select anyone to represent you?"

Claudette looked away for a moment and thought it over. Returning his gaze, she spoke slowly. "Quite naturally we are not going to have any ignorant person to lead us . . . We had to have someone who is strong enough to speak up . . . someone who knows the law . . . It is quite natural that we are not going to get up there ourselves [when] some of [us] can't even read or write . . . But they knew they were treated wrong."

Knabe sprang his trap—or tried to.

"Is the Reverend King the one you selected?"

"We didn't elect him."

"You *said* you selected somebody who was better informed to represent you. Now who did you select?"

"Well, I don't know anything about selections, but we all just got together."

"But *somebody* spoke for your group," Knabe insisted. "Now who was it?"

"I don't know," Claudette said. "We all spoke for ourselves."

Knabe wouldn't let go. "Now just a minute ago I understood you to say that you *selected* somebody that knew the law better. Now who was that person?"

Claudette widened her eyes. "Who knew the law better? A lot of people know the law better. Now, are you trying to say that Dr. King was the leader of the whole thing?"

Knabe rubbed his head, seemingly in exasperation. Then, drawing the syllables out one at a time, as if speaking to a small child, he said, "I am merely asking if Reverend King was one of the leaders who represented your group at that time, and expressed to the city commission what the Negroes wanted."

"Probably," Claudette replied, "but I don't know."

Knabe switched tacks. "Now, was Attorney Gray here one of those whom you felt knew the laws?"

"Yes, quite naturally . . . He is a lawyer."

"Did you know at the time," Knabe said, voice rising, "that he sustained that the state law didn't apply at all in the city of Montgomery?"

Claudette shook her head dismissively. "I go to school myself and I know there is a lot of law, state law, national law, and local law."

Knabe asked the judges to instruct Claudette to answer questions more directly. Judge Rives told her, "If you know the answers just say 'yes' or 'no.' Don't make speeches."

So for the next few minutes Claudette answered all of Knabe's questions with one word or the other, yes or no. She broke her pattern only when Knabe finally asked her the question that went right to the heart of the matter.

"Why did you stop riding the buses on December fifth?"

"Because," Claudette answered, her gaze level and her voice even and intense, "we were treated wrong, dirty and nasty."

Spectators in the crowd murmured yeses in response.

Knabe had had enough. "No further questions," he said. Claudette got up and returned to her seat. Charles Langford, one of the lawyers for the plaintiffs, was deeply impressed by her presentation. "If there was a star witness in the boycott case," he later told the writer Frank Sikora, "it had to be Claudette Colvin."

• • •

CLAUDETTE: Soon after I testified there was a noon recess. Jo Ann Robinson came up and took Mary Louise Smith and me to H. L. Green's, a five-and-ten-cent store, for lunch. I had never met Mary Louise before, and I hadn't heard her bus story until that morning. We sat there eating and comparing notes about what had happened to us. I liked Mary Louise and I was proud that two teenaged girls had stood up.

• • •

AFTER LUNCH, testimony resumed. Mayor Gayle and several city commissioners insisted the segregation laws were needed to maintain order in the city. One commissioner, Clyde Sellers, warned, "If segregation barriers are lifted, violence will be the order of the day."

Judge Rives thought this over for a moment in the silent courtroom. Then he asked Sellers, "Can you command one man to surrender his constitutional rights—if they are his constitutional rights—to prevent another man from committing a crime?"

Sellers had no answer to that. The hearing was adjourned in late afternoon.

• • •

CLAUDETTE: When I came out of the courthouse, I was surrounded by adults. Everyone was shaking my hand. I was squeamish of people taking my hand and touching me, but I did like it when they said, "Oh, yes, you were great."

I went back up to King Hill. Raymond was still asleep, and Mama Sweetie said, "He must have known you were up to something good because he didn't give us one moment's trouble."

I described the whole thing to Mom over dinner. A. C. James came over from across the street and said, "You really spoke out!" Mom was proud of me. I felt relieved. I called my biological mom in Birmingham and my uncle C. J. McNear. Mom telephoned Reverend Johnson and said, "It's over. Claudette has testified."

I called some of my schoolmates that I was still in touch with, and then rocked Raymond until he went to sleep. Finally I was alone with my thoughts. I was exhausted, but proud. I had been preparing for this in my head for three months. The questions seemed obvious by the time I heard them. I had looked white officials in the eye and stood up for my people. I felt I had done my best. Now it was up to the judges.

I looked over at Raymond, fast asleep in his bassinet, and I said, "I think I might have done us some good today."

The Bell Street Baptist Church was reduced to rubble by a bomb
thrown three weeks after Montgomery's city buses were integrated

CHAPTER TEN

RAGE IN MONTGOMERY

Is Montgomery to be a city in which bullets fly between sundown and sunup?
—From an editorial in the *Montgomery Advertiser*, January 1957

A S THE COURTROOM was being cleared of spectators, the three robed men went into Judge Johnson's chambers, shut the door, and sat down. No one said anything for a while. Then Judge Rives said to Johnson, "Frank, you're the junior judge here. You vote first. What do you think?"

Johnson replied, "Judge, as far as I'm concerned, state-imposed segregation on public facilities [the buses] violates the Constitution. I'm going to rule with the plaintiffs here." Justice Rives quickly agreed. Justice Lynne didn't. "The [Supreme] Court has already spoken on this issue in *Plessy versus Ferguson*," he insisted. "It's the law and we're bound by it until it's changed." But Lynne was outnumbered. By a 2–1 decision a federal court abolished segregated seating on Montgomery's—and Alabama's—buses. As Judge Johnson later said, "The testimony of . . . Miss Colvin and the others reinforced the Constitution's position that you can't abridge the freedoms of the individual. The boycott case was a simple case of legal and human rights being denied."

The decision, which took all of ten minutes to make, was announced on June 19, 1956. Shocked, Mayor Gayle declared that the city would appeal the case to the U.S. Supreme Court. But protesters rejoiced in a mass meeting at the Holt Street Baptist Church, a celebration tempered by the realization that they would have to keep walking at least until the city's appeal reached Washington. The case probably wouldn't be considered until fall. And there was no guarantee even then that the Supreme Court would agree with the Alabama judges.

The day after the court's announcement, Judge Johnson opened an envelope from the morning's mail and unfolded an unsigned letter. It read:

> If I had been in your shoes before I would have ruled [*sic*] as you did, I would rather have had my right arm cut off. I trust that you will get on your knees and pray to Almighty God to forgive you for the mistake that you have made.

It was just the first of many hate-filled letters and phone calls he would soon receive.

• • •

CLAUDETTE: I heard about the court decision on the news. Nobody called to tell me. By then I didn't have much time for celebrating anyway. I had been kicked out of school and I had a three-month-old baby. My dream of

WHAT THE JUDGES SAID IN *BROWDER V. GAYLE*

Writing for the majority, Judges Johnson and Rives said:

We hold that the statutes and ordinances requiring segregation of the white and colored races on the motor buses of a common carrier of passengers in the city of Montgomery and its police jurisdictions . . . [violate] the due process and equal protection of the law . . . under the Fourteenth Amendment of the Constitution of the United States.

The "separate but equal" doctrine set forth by the Supreme Court in 1896 in the case of Plessy v. Ferguson *can no longer be applied.*

being a lawyer was gone. I needed money so badly, and I was worn out trying to figure out how to get my life back.

When you're a teenager and you first get pregnant, you can't understand the reality of raising a child, especially if you don't have the father to help out or even talk to you. I had no idea how much work there would be and how much money I would need. I didn't have to pay rent to Mom and Dad, but I did have to pay for food and clothing and help with utility bills. My dad wasn't working, and my mom made three dollars a day.

Judge Frank M. Johnson, Jr. "The strength of the Constitution," he said, "lies in its flexibility"

I hoped maybe some of the boycott leaders would understand my situation and help me, after what I had done. Deep inside I hoped maybe they would give me a baby shower. I needed money and support so badly. But I didn't hear from any of them after I left the courthouse. Not Fred Gray. Not Rosa Parks. Not Jo Ann Robinson. No one called after I testified. I knew they couldn't put me up onstage like the queen of the boycott, but after what I had done, why did they have to turn their backs on me?

I knew the answer: I was shunned because I had gotten pregnant. It was made worse because my parents wouldn't let me just explain, "This is what happened and here's who the father is." Anyone could have understood, but I had promised my parents, so I kept it to myself. But because Raymond was light-skinned, and I wouldn't name the father, they all assumed the father was white. Socially, I had three strikes against me: I was an unmarried teenager with a light-skinned baby. Without school, I had no circle of friends my age, and there was no way any of the women in town would accept me. To them I was a fallen woman.

But I wasn't ashamed of myself. I knew I wasn't a bad person. A more experienced and much older man took advantage of me when I was at my very lowest. I got caught up in a mistake, yes, but that's all it was—a mistake. The people closest to me didn't give up on me. They held on to me. Q.P. and Mary Ann loved me, and so did Mama Sweetie and Velma. They never forgot the good things about me. My pastor, Reverend Johnson, supported me. And Baby Tell, my mom's best friend from Pine Level, was wonderful. Every second Sunday during my pregnancy I would go out in the country and stay with her. She would make the bed for me and read me to sleep from the Bible. She made a long little flannel gown for my baby, embroidered all the way around with the colors of the rainbow. And of course I had Raymond. He was a happy little fella. I was loved.

When the court decision came down, of course I felt joy for my people and pride for what I had done, but my day-to-day problems overwhelmed me. The thing that was constantly in the front of my mind was: How can I get started again? How in this world can I pick myself up?

• • •

THROUGHOUT THE SUMMER OF 1956, Montgomery's mayor, councilors, and other officials tried everything they could to crush the boycott. They singled out Dr. King among the 115 blacks who had received indictments and went after him, accusing him of organizing an illegal boycott. The NAACP sent reinforcements from New York to help Fred Gray and other local attorneys defend Dr. King, but it was no use. Dr. King was found guilty by Judge Eugene Carter, the same judge who had ruled in Claudette's appeal. Carter sentenced King to pay five hundred dollars and serve one year of hard labor in prison.

Reporters flocked to Montgomery from all over the world to report the dramatic racial showdown. Some frustrated whites complained that their leaders were all talk and that it was time to take matters into their own hands. If they didn't act now, blacks would soon control the city. On the sweltering night of August 25, 1956, someone lit the fuse to several sticks of dynamite and lobbed them into the front yard of the Reverend Robert S. Graetz, the white pastor of Trinity Lutheran Church. The blast shattered the windows and rocked the walls of houses throughout the neighborhood. The Graetz family was spared only because they were away.

Summer and early fall brought more terror, more death threats, more hate mail and midnight phone calls—and frustration. Segregationists never seemed to run out of ideas or the money to carry them out. The White Citizens Council sought to pull insurance coverage from the MIA's fleet of station wagons. City officials asked a state court to ban the car pool, claiming it was an unlicensed transportation system.

On Tuesday, November 13, Dr. King and other leaders sat in a courtroom, dejectedly listening to the city's lawyers tell a clearly sympathetic judge that the boycott was illegal and should be outlawed. During a recess in the trial, Dr. King turned around and noticed Mayor Gayle, Commissioner Sellers, and two attorneys quickly disappearing into a back room. Several reporters hustled in and out of the same room. Something strange was going on.

Then one of the reporters walked up to King and handed him a news bulletin that had just come in. King read it and later wrote, "My heart began to throb with inexpressible joy." The U.S. Supreme Court had just affirmed the lower court's ruling in *Browder v. Gayle*. They had won! Word

∕GETTING TO SIT WHEREVER YOU WANTED

"I rode the bus with my aunt on the very first day," recalls Annie Larkin, who was then sixteen. "We took the Highland Gardens bus that morning and I sat right up front. I had been following the boycott all the way through—I had only missed maybe five mass meetings in the whole year, so I wanted to ride on the very first day. I felt elated, I could sit anywhere I wanted."

Gwendolyn Patton was fourteen when she moved from Detroit to Montgomery in 1960. She was well aware of the historic bus victory and proud to plop herself in a seat up front among white passengers whenever she rode the bus. But she found it puzzling that her grandmother still walked to the back to find her seat. One day Gwendolyn asked her about it. Her grandmother answered that she preferred to sit in the back. "Darling," she explained, "the bus boycott was not about sitting next to white people. It was about sitting anywhere you please."

raced through the courtroom. One man rose and shouted, "God Almighty has spoken from Washington, D.C.!" Judge Carter banged his gavel for order. And then, in one last, utterly futile gesture, Carter ruled that the MIA car pool was illegal and must stop operating. It was all beside the point now. A team of creative lawyers and four tough women—two of them teenagers—had just booted Jim Crow off the buses.

Mayor Gayle vowed that the city would hold out until the very end, meaning until someone representing the United States actually showed up in Montgomery and delivered the Supreme Court's order to integrate the buses. And now, because of Judge Carter's ruling, the boycott was illegal. At a mass meeting, King announced that, until the Supreme Court's order arrived, "we will continue to walk and share rides with friends." He supposed it would take "three or four days."

Five weeks later, on December 20—381 days after the boycott had started—two federal marshals arrived at the federal courthouse and served written notices on city officials that Montgomery's buses had to be integrated. "I guess we'll have to abide by it," Mayor Gayle sighed, "because it's the law."

Many boycott participants would forever remember where they were when they heard the news. "I was cooking . . . when they made the an-

December 21, 1956, the first day of integrated bus service in Montgomery: (front) Rev. Ralph Abernathy and Inez Baskin of the *Montgomery Advertiser*; (back) Rev. Martin Luther King, Jr., and Rev. Glenn Smiley

A demolitions expert carefully defuses a bomb in the
tense aftermath of *Browder v. Gayle*

nouncement on the radio," recalled Georgia Gilmore. "I ran outside and
there was my neighbor and she said yes, and we were so happy. We . . . had
accomplished something that no one ever thought would happen in the city
of Montgomery. Being able to ride the bus and sit anyplace that you desire."

At 5:55 the next morning, Dr. King and four other leaders, none of
whom were plaintiffs in *Browder v. Gayle*, stepped aboard the open door to
an empty bus at a stop near King's home and dropped coins into the fare
box. When the white bus driver recognized the famous man coming through
the door, he smiled and said, "I believe you are Reverend King, aren't you?"

"Yes, I am," King answered.

"We are glad to have you this morning," said the driver.

With that, the bus protest ignited by Claudette's arrest twenty-one
months earlier came to an end. It was one of the great human rights vic-
tories in U.S. history. But many years later one writer noticed something
peculiar about that first bus ride. "It is interesting," puzzled Frank Sikora
in his book *The Judge*, "that Claudette Colvin was not in the group."

• • •

Browder v. Gayle may have ended legal segregation on the buses, but
it did not end racial prejudice. Less than a week after the buses were

integrated, five white men jumped out of a car at a Montgomery bus stop and surrounded a fifteen-year-old black girl. Cursing her, they beat her to the ground and sped away. Four days later a second young black woman, named Rosa Jordan, was shot in both legs while riding the Boylston bus by a sniper whose bullets penetrated the vehicle. Around the same time, Aurelia Browder's daughter Manervia ran to answer the phone ringing late in the night. "Your house is gonna be blowed sky high!" a voice said. She became hysterical. Her mother grabbed the phone and told the caller, "Blow it up. I need a new house, anyway!" and slammed the phone down.

Violence and threats of revenge were everywhere in the first days of integrated buses. Annie Larkin remembers being in a mass meeting at a church soon after the Supreme Court's decision. "We had gotten there at four p.m. to get a good seat. But while the meeting was going on people came and set fire to the cars parked out in front of the church. No one would let us out until it was safe. A guard unit ended up escorting us home about four a.m."

Montgomery turned into a battle zone on the night of January 10, 1957, as bombs rocked the city's black churches. Claudette's church, Hutchinson Street Baptist, was dynamited, its stained-glass windows blown to pieces. The Bell Street Baptist Church was bombed, too, as was Reverend Abernathy's home. Terrorists once again bombed the home of Reverend Graetz—especially despised by many as a white clergyman who openly supported black rights. All in all, four churches and two houses were damaged by explosives that night. Another bomb tossed onto Dr. King's front yard somehow failed to go off.

It was clear that anyone connected to the boycott, anyone whose name or picture had been in the paper—was now in grave danger. Q. P. Colvin, planted in his chair on King Hill, stayed close to his shotgun. The *Montgomery Advertiser* summed up the first days of 1957 with a blunt editorial: "The issue now has passed beyond segregation. The issue now is whether it is safe to live in Montgomery, Alabama."

• • •

CLAUDETTE: I was afraid, but I couldn't just hide at home. I had to work. I needed money. I decided I would be safer in restaurants than in white people's homes—you never knew who was KKK. But whenever I'd start a job in a cafeteria, word would get around fast about who I was. Sometimes black people would recognize me and come up and embrace me and say, "You the girl!" I got fired from several restaurant jobs when my employers found out I was the one who wouldn't give up her seat. I'd change my name back and forth from Colvin to Austin so I could work, but they'd always find out and that was that. It was hard for me to remain anonymous.

No one with any pull would help me or hire me. Those were hard, fearsome days: In those days, it seemed like I couldn't go anywhere and no one wanted to be near me. I wanted to escape from there.

There was one small good thing that happened right after the boycott ended. One afternoon Reverend Ralph Abernathy, the pastor of the First Baptist Church, called our house and invited me to a private reception there. Abernathy knew Velma because she was a member. I decided to go. There weren't very many people invited, just a few from ASC, and a reporter, and Velma and I, and the Kings and Abernathys.

Dr. King sat near the door, always surrounded by people. Reverend Abernathy stayed close to him. After a while, I got up and went in the kitchen to help Mrs. Abernathy serve ice cream. I carried a scoop out to Dr. King, still sitting by the door. I had never met him before except to shake his hand in line after a mass meeting. I had always been too shy to approach him. Usually there were too many people around him to get near anyway.

When he saw me, he stood and introduced himself and thanked me for being in the court case. He said, "You're a brave young lady." I told him I was trying to get back to school, and he listened with interest. It wasn't a long conversation; I moved on quickly. But it was important to me. How could you not respect him? King put his life on the line and didn't have to. Because he stood up, his life was always in danger, more so than the other ministers'. His speeches at the mass meetings kept people walking and kept things from getting out of control.

Meeting Dr. King didn't pay my bills or stop people from gossiping about me and Raymond. It sure didn't make me any safer. But I have to say those few words of praise from him on that evening felt very good.

Claudette Colvin, February 2005, speaking to students
at Booker T. Washington Magnet High School

EPILOGUE

HISTORY'S DOOR

Claudette Colvin had more courage, in my opinion,
than any of the [other] persons involved in the movement.
—Fred Gray

February 2005, Booker T. Washington Magnet High School,
Montgomery, Alabama

TWO HUNDRED JUNIORS AND SENIORS—about half white and half black, with a smattering of students from other racial and ethnic backgrounds—file into the school auditorium for a midmorning assembly. They settle into seats and squint at the stage, where a small group of black women are seated.

Lights dim, and a youthful figure wearing a simple dress and horn-rimmed glasses takes center stage. The actress and storyteller Awele Makeba transforms the auditorium into a packed city bus, the scene of a tense standoff between a determined black girl and several uniformed white men. Students in the audience lean forward, absorbed, maybe asking themselves if they would have taken such risks, and wondering how they would have held up under such pressure.

When the performance is finished, the principal turns to a woman who has not moved throughout the performance and invites her forward. She rises slowly and takes a few steps up to the microphone and into the light. The students of Booker T. Washington High, blacks and whites together, rise to cheer her. Though the woman smiles warmly, there are no tears.

"Do you have any questions?" Claudette Colvin asks the students.

It has been a long way back home.

•

In 1957, the year after *Browder v. Gayle*, Claudette passed her G.E.D. and then enrolled at Alabama State College. Dissatisfied with the courses offered, she dropped out after a year.

Unable to find work in Montgomery, in 1958 Claudette followed Velma to New York City, reluctantly leaving Raymond in the care of her mom. At first she felt caged in by New York. "I would wake up in the night in Velma's tiny little apartment thinking I was in that cell in Montgomery," she remembers. "Sometimes I thought I could hear the jailer's key."

Claudette gave birth to a second son, Randy, in 1960. Unsure about how best to help her boys—trying to raise them on a maid's salary in Montgomery or sending money home from her New York job as a live-in family caregiver—she went "back and forth like a yo-yo" until, in 1968, she finally settled in New York. Claudette received nurse's training and took a job as a nurse's aide in a Catholic hospital in New York, where she cared for elderly patients, often at night. She worked there for many years.

During the 1960s, Claudette kept up with the civil rights movement in the news but stayed on the sidelines. Caution had become a habit; she told no one of her activist past. Decade by decade, she watched Rosa Parks's fame grow as the person who had ignited the movement by refusing to surrender her seat to a white passenger on a bus in Montgomery, Alabama. Sometimes she wondered if anyone back home even remembered her arrest and testimony. *Browder v. Gayle*, overshadowed by the more famous school case, *Brown v. Board of Education of Topeka*, was rarely mentioned in histories of the movement. The names of the four women who took down the bus segregation laws seemed to have been forgotten. The door to her place in history seemed closed forever.

And then, unexpectedly, it cracked open. In 1975 Frank Sikora, a Birmingham newspaper reporter writing a story on the Montgomery bus boycott, thought he remembered there had been someone *before* Rosa Parks. Library research brought up a name: Claudette Colvin. Flipping through the Montgomery phone book, Sikora found a Q. P. Colvin still listed at the address mentioned in one of the old stories. He grabbed his notebook, drove to King Hill, and pulled up to a small frame house. "I was met at the door by a woman of about seventy, slender and with a face full of dignity," he remembers. "It was Mary Ann Colvin, the woman who raised Claudette. I interviewed her and asked if she had a picture of Claudette. She dug out a little school snapshot, and scribbled down a phone number in New York City."

Sikora telephoned a surprised Claudette and wrote a story about her. A few more stories followed, as well as chapters in two books about children of the civil rights movement. Her name began to appear in histories of the movement, though Claudette Colvin was usually presented as a feisty, immature teenager who got arrested before Rosa Parks but was "not the right person" to be a boycott leader. Many accounts said that Claudette was pregnant at the time she was arrested. "That would have been the first thirteen-month pregnancy in history," Claudette observes. She kept her phone number unlisted and turned down most offers to speak.

But she did accept the offer of a ticket back home in 2005. The *Montgomery Advertiser* was sponsoring a fiftieth anniversary commemoration of the Montgomery bus boycott. People really seemed to want her to come. Friends would be there, as well as many of the activists still alive. And so it was that now, as part of that remembrance, she found herself standing before the students of Booker T. Washington, the very school from which she had been expelled a half century before.

• • •

CLAUDETTE: How did it feel? Awesome. Wonderful. It felt like young people hadn't abandoned the cause, like they really wanted to know what we went through. They appreciated what we did to try to clear the way for them. A black girl and a white girl stood on either side of me and we had our photograph taken together. I told them that years ago it would have been unheard of for a white student and a black student to be standing together, and learning together on an equal basis. It seemed unbelievable that this had come to pass.

We had a question-and-answer session, and they asked what I would say to them, looking back from my years. I told them: Don't give up. Keep struggling, and don't slide back. Grab all the resources that are available for you, and get yourselves ready to compete. I told them to take their education seriously.

I know that segregation isn't dead—just look at schools and neighborhoods and workplaces, and you can see that it's still all over America. And yes, we are still at the very beginning economically. But at least those degrading signs, "White" and "Colored," are gone. We destroyed them. There are laws now that make segregation illegal. We forced white people to take a different view. They had to change their attitude toward blacks. The civil rights movement cleared the way legally so we could progress. It opened the doors for the younger generation. I'm glad I was a part of that.

When I look back now, I think Rosa Parks was the right person to represent that movement at that time. She was a good and strong person, accepted by more people than were ready to accept me. But I made a personal statement, too, one that she didn't make and probably couldn't have made. Mine was the first cry for justice, and a loud one. I made it so that our own adult leaders couldn't just be nice anymore. Back then, as a teenager, I kept thinking, Why don't the adults around here just say something? Say it so they know we don't accept segregation? I knew then and I know now that, when it comes to justice, there is no easy way to get it. You can't sugarcoat it. You have to take a stand and say, "This is not right."

And I did.

AUTHOR'S NOTE

In the year 2000, while I was writing my book *We Were There, Too!: Young People in U.S. History*, someone told me that a fifteen-year-old African-American girl had taken the same defiant stand as Rosa Parks, in the same city, but almost a year earlier. As the story went, this girl's refusal to give up her seat on a city bus to a white passenger had helped inspire the famous Montgomery, Alabama, bus boycott of 1955 and 1956. But instead of being honored, she had been shunned by her classmates, dismissed as an unfit role model by adult leaders, and later overlooked by historians.

An Internet search led me to the name Claudette Colvin. I found that, indeed, in March 1955, this high school junior had been arrested, dragged backwards off the bus by police, handcuffed, and jailed for refusing to surrender her bus seat to a white passenger. Her protest had taken place almost nine months to the day before Rosa Parks had famously taken the same stand.

Reading on, I discovered that Claudette Colvin didn't give up after she was arrested and tried. A year later, she and three other women *sued* the city of Montgomery and the state of Alabama, challenging the laws requiring segregated seating on buses. Only after they won, in a case known as *Browder v. Gayle*, were the city's buses integrated.

Is Claudette Colvin still alive? I asked myself. If so, where is she? Further research turned up a 1995 article about her in *USA Today*, framing Ms. Colvin as an important but nearly forgotten civil rights pioneer. Her obscurity, said the writer, was the product of "shyness, missed communications and a historical bum rap." The article said Ms. Colvin was now fifty-six years old and living in New York City, where she worked at a private nursing home.

I telephoned the reporter, Richard Willing, who said yes, he was still in touch with Ms. Colvin. After we talked, he agreed to contact her to see if she would be interested in working with me on a book about her early life.

For the next four years, Mr. Willing called Claudette Colvin occasionally on my behalf. Always the message relayed back to me was "Maybe when I retire." I had all but given up when, one night in the fall of 2006, I saw the red light blinking on my answering machine. It was Richard Willing. His message was brief: "Claudette says I can give you her phone number," he said. "Here it is. Good luck."

Soon after that night, I rang the bell of Claudette Colvin's apartment in a New York high-rise apartment building. The door was pulled open by a caramel-colored woman who greeted me with a shy smile as she inspected me closely through wide-framed glasses. She had a nest of curls on top of her head. We walked—she with the aid of a cane—to a restaurant that had a quiet room where we could talk over a meal. She laughed easily and spoke in a tuneful voice that still had plenty of Montgomery in it but had also taken on a Caribbean lilt, since some of her New York neighbors were Jamaicans. We decided to work together.

During the following year Claudette shared the personal history of a dramatic social revolution. Having played a central role in events that helped destroy the legal basis for racial segregation in the United States, she still remembered not only what happened but how it felt. She could still describe the inside of her cell, the sound of a jailer's key, and the view from a witness box in a packed federal courtroom. She could also remember the rage she felt when the adults in her life complained at home about segregation but accepted it outside.

In fourteen long interviews during the next year—three in New York and the others by telephone—I asked Claudette thousands of questions. Only a very few times did she gesture for me to turn the tape recorder off, or say she would prefer to keep something to herself. She gave me the telephone numbers of friends and family members, and encouraged them to talk to me. She was wonderfully open and generous.

More than any other story I know, Claudette Colvin's life story shows how history is made up of objective facts and personal truths, braided together. In her case, a girl raised in poverty by a strong, loving family twice risked her life to gain a measure of justice for her people. Hers is the story of a wise and brave woman who, when she was a smart, angry teenager in Jim Crow Alabama, made contributions to human rights far too important to be forgotten.

AFTERWORD

In the past year Claudette Colvin and I have made numerous appearances together at schools and libraries. I have been keeping a list of the questions most commonly asked of Claudette at these events. The opportunity to write a new afterword for this paperback edition gave me a chance to ask them myself in a telephone interview with Claudette Colvin on August 9, 2010.

PH: After you moved from Montgomery to New York City, you went decades without telling anyone about your activity in the civil rights movement. Why did you keep it quiet?
CC: Some of the first people I met in New York were followers of Malcolm X. They didn't agree with Dr. King's philosophy of nonviolent change. Malcolm's people were speaking very aggressively about making change "by any means necessary." That included armed violence. Having grown up in the South and having lived through the Montgomery bus boycott, I knew you couldn't just go down there with guns. And besides, I didn't have time to be politically active: I was busy trying to support my family and getting all the overtime I could get.

PH: As Rosa Parks became more famous and you remained silent, did you assume your story would just fade and die?

CC: I didn't know whether anyone back in Montgomery remembered me or not. I completely lost touch with the leaders of the boycott. I didn't think the black historians in Montgomery wanted my story out there. The historian at Alabama State College seemed to want professionals to get all the credit for success in Montgomery. I don't think the leaders wanted people to know that the first cry came from a teenager and the second came from another, Mary Louise Smith. They wanted Rosa Parks to go down in history as the icon. I was especially disappointed that the elite didn't seem to want anyone to know about *Browder v. Gayle*, the lawsuit that ended the boycott. In most books about it, all you see is this picture of Dr. Martin Luther King and Ralph Abernathy on the bus with a white passenger. Looking at it, you'd think that the boycott had won over the bus company. They don't tell about all the litigation that went down.

PH: You broke your silence when a reporter from Birmingham called you in 1980. Were you surprised when that call came?

CC: Really surprised. My mom had called first to tell me that a newspaper reporter named Frank Sikora had visited her house, wanting a picture of me. She gave him the photo and my number and said I should be expecting his call. He telephoned, explaining that the twenty-fifth anniversary of the boycott was approaching and he was doing a story on it. He wondered if anyone had invited me down for the event. I told him no, I hadn't heard a thing about it.

PH: Was it a relief to finally talk about it to somebody?

CC: I suppose, but it was mostly disappointing to hear that none of the black leaders had invited me down to the boycott anniversary.

PH: Did you find New York City to be a lot different from the South?

CC: Oh yes. The very first day, I got off the bus at the Port Authority with all my bags in my hands and started to go into a drugstore. A white man held the door open for me. I just stood there and couldn't move for a moment. I was stunned. That had never happened down South.

PH: What kind of work did you do in New York?
CC: For thirty-six years I worked in a Catholic nursing home in Manhattan. My co-workers were from all over the world. I provided day-to-day care for elderly patients. Some were paralyzed with strokes. Some were blind. I took care of their physical and social needs. I learned a lot from the patients. One taught me about painting, about the different periods of art, like the impressionists. Others were able to help me understand patients with speech impediments.

PH: Readers were introduced to your son Raymond when he was a baby. What has his life been like since?
CC: He started out as a happy little fella, but from first grade on, when he realized that people put a value on light skin, he grew to hate school. Raymond grew up in the South. He visited me but he never did come to New York to live. He was restless. After the Army he became a drifter, flipping burgers, doing construction work. His life ended when he overdosed. He died in March 1993 at the age of thirty-seven. Raymond has a son, Quinyardo. I have a good connection with him. Raymond knew about my civil rights actions and he was proud of me. He was always saying, "Mom, why don't you *tell* someone? A lot of people in Montgomery don't know that you were before Rosa." He said nobody believed him when he told them.

PH: You have another son, too.
CC: Yes, my life had calmed down by the time I had Randy. He was more stable and had a long attention span. He made good grades all the way through school. He's an accountant now, and he has four children: Christine, Jennifer, Randy II, and Jamal.

PH: Did Rosa Parks ever try to contact you after you left Alabama?
CC: She called me once, in the late 1980s. She said she was giving a speech at Manhattan Community College and she invited me to come hear

her. She didn't make any conversation, just a blunt invitation. I thought it over for a while, but even if I'd wanted to go, Rosa didn't give me enough time to put in for a day off from work. I wasn't going to call in sick just to hear her speak. I thought she should have had more diplomacy, that she should have said more to me after all those years. I might have been interested if she was offering me a chance to tell my side of the story, but it was nothing like that. I don't know what she was thinking. I didn't know her mind.

PH: I tried for several years to reach you about writing a book, but you kept saying, "Maybe when I retire." Why were you reluctant?
CC: I didn't want to risk my job. I didn't want to be forced to resign because of fame or something. I had worked so long and hard, I wanted to get my full retirement before I turned to anything else. My co-workers had already been shocked once when a story about me and Mary Louise Smith came out in *USA Today* in 1995. There was my photo, right on the cover. They couldn't believe it. I was always considered a softy by the other workers. And as for working with you, I didn't know how far you were going or how far the book would go. I didn't want any confusion on the job.

PH: Was it hard for you to entrust your story to a white author?
CC: People ask me that all the time: "Why didn't you get a black author to write your story?" Well, for one thing, no black author approached me. I would have had to pay someone. And then after I retired, when you contacted me, I thought, Why not? I figured if Frank Sikora and Richard Willing (the *USA Today* reporter) and Ellen Levine, who interviewed me in the early days and wrote about me in a book called *Freedom's Children*, had told the truth, you could tell it too. The truth is the truth regardless of the color of the author.

PH: Do you like the way the book turned out?
CC: Yes, I do. I didn't know you'd put so much time into the book, or that you would go into such detail about my life. I thought you were just picking up on a story, maybe building on what the *USA Today* article had done

years before. I didn't know you'd be that dedicated to the story. You're more than what I thought you were going to be, and so is the book. My son Randy said you just lifted me up and placed me into history.

PH: Has fame changed anything for you?
CC: It's nice to get some recognition. The best part has been talking to young people. I meet more children now, and they can use my story to see that it really was a struggle to win our civil rights. The appearances give me a chance to tell children that without an education they can't go anyplace. Not if you're from a minority group. You're stuck. If you have a dream, you need an education. It's the same way now as when I was going to Booker T. Washington High School in Montgomery. I tell my grandchildren the truth: "This is a capitalist country and money counts."

PH: One thing hasn't changed. You're still hard to find.
CC: Yeah, I like to keep a low profile. I tell people, too, that just because you won the National Book Award doesn't mean the book is on the bestseller list or that I'm rich. I don't want people pushing their way into my apartment thinking I've got money.

PH: When you were young, you wanted to be a lawyer but you weren't able to go to law school. Looking back, do you still think that would have been a good fit for you?
CC: Yes. I would have been a civil lawyer, not a criminal lawyer. There's still a lot of legal work out there to be done. Sometimes when you get a title like "attorney," people will listen to you more. I think I could have gotten a word in.

BIBLIOGRAPHY

I consulted hundreds of Web sites, articles, and books in writing about Claudette. These titles were among the most helpful.

BOOKS

Branch, Taylor. *Parting the Waters: America in the King Years, 1954–63.* New York: Simon & Schuster, 1988.

Garrow, David J. *Bearing the Cross: Martin Luther King, Jr., and the Southern Christian Leadership Conference.* New York: Vintage Books, 1986.

Gray, Fred D. *Bus Ride to Justice: Changing the System by the System.* Montgomery, Ala.: Black Belt Press, 1995. In this autobiography, Claudette's lawyer, Fred Gray, offers his account of using the law to "destroy everything segregated I could find."

Halberstam, David. *The Fifties*. New York: Villard Books, 1993.

Hampton, Henry, and Steve Fayer. *Voices of Freedom: An Oral History of the Civil Rights Movement*. New York: Bantam Books, 1990. This book contains interviews with Montgomery residents who led or took part in the boycott.

Hare, Kenneth M., ed. *They Walked to Freedom: The Story of the Montgomery Bus Boycott*. Champaign, Ill.: Spotlight Press L.L.C., 2005. This book was published by the *Montgomery Advertiser* to mark the fiftieth anniversary of the Montgomery bus boycott. Profiles, photos, and news stories of the time are included.

King, Martin Luther, Jr. *Stride Toward Freedom: The Montgomery Story*. New York: Harper & Row, 1958. Dr. King's account of the bus protest.

Levine, Ellen. *Freedom's Children: Young Civil Rights Activists Tell Their Own Stories*. New York: G. P. Putnam's Sons, 1993. Ms. Levine interviewed Claudette as part of this excellent volume.

Newman, Richard, and Marcia Sawyer. *Everybody Say Freedom: Everything You Need to Know about African-American History*. New York: Penguin Books, 1996.

Robinson, Jo Ann Gibson. *The Montgomery Bus Boycott and the Women Who Started It*. Knoxville: University of Tennessee Press, 1987. This wonderful book is especially valuable in documenting the abuse that blacks experienced while simply getting from place to place during the bus boycott.

Sikora, Frank. *The Judge: The Life and Opinions of Alabama's Frank M. Johnson, Jr.* Montgomery, Ala.: Black Belt Press, 1992. Sikora, a former reporter for *The Birmingham News*, has done a great deal to keep Claudette's name from simply disappearing. He tracked her parents down during the 1970s and wrote the first newspaper story about her contributions to U.S. history. In *The Judge*, he recovered and published parts of the transcript of the *Browder v. Gayle* hearing, allowing us to hear Claudette's actual words and filling in Judge Johnson's impressions of her testimony. He provided the basis for my book's Chapter 9.

Williams, Donnie, with Wayne Greenhaw. *The Thunder of Angels: The Montgomery Bus Boycott and the People Who Broke the Back of Jim Crow.* Chicago: Lawrence Hill Books, 2006. This book offers a very good portrait of a troubled Montgomery in the months after the bus boycott ended.

Williams, Juan. *Eyes on the Prize: America's Civil Rights Years, 1954–1965.* New York: Penguin Books, 1988.

ARTICLES

Garrow, David J. "The Origins of the Montgomery Bus Boycott." *Southern Changes* 7, no. 5 (1985): 21–27.

Johnson, Robert E. "Bombing, Harassment Don't Stop Foot-Weary Negro Boycotters." *Jet*, February 16, 1956, 8–13.

King, M. L., Jr. "Statement Delivered at the Prayer Pilgrimage Protesting the Electrocution of Jeremiah Reeves." From *The Papers of Martin Luther King, Jr.*, vol. IV: *Symbol of a Movement, January 1957–December 1958*, April 6, 1958. http://mlk-kpp01.stanford.edu/primarydocuments/Vol4/6-Apr-1958_JeremiahReevesStatement.pdf

"Negroes Stop Riding Montgomery Buses in Protest over Jim Crow." *Jet*, December 22, 1955, 12–15.

Thornton, J. Mills, III. "Challenge and Response in the Montgomery Bus Boycott of 1955–6." *Alabama Review* 33 (July 1980): 163–235.

Willing, Richard. "Then Teens, They 'Stood Up for Something.' " *USA Today*, November 28, 1995. A long, well-written front-page story about Claudette Colvin and Mary Louise Smith.

Younge, Gary. "She Would Not Be Moved." *The Guardian*, December 16, 2000.

SELECTED WEB SITES

www.ferris.edu/jimcrow/ will take you to the Jim Crow Museum of Racist Memorabilia. Here you can inspect an array of objects, signs, cartoons, and other materials related to racial segregation and civil rights.

www.riversofchange.org is the Internet address for a fine set of educational materials on *Browder v. Gayle* and the plaintiffs, including Claudette. The DVD, curriculum guide, and workbook emphasize rights that were re-captured by the landmark decision.

mlk-kpp01.stanford.edu is the Web site for the Martin Luther King, Jr., Research and Education Institute at Stanford University. Especially help-ful to educators is the "Liberation Curriculum," presenting a wide range of materials related to the African-American freedom struggle.

NOTES

The "Claudette" sections come from a series of fourteen interviews I conducted with Claudette Colvin between January 1 and September 13, 2007. Three of these interviews took place in person in New York City, the others by telephone. Almost all lasted more than an hour, and those in New York extended through much of the day. We also had many shorter conversations, when I would call her to clarify something or ask another question or two. Finally, Claudette let me read aloud the text of the entire book to her, sometimes stopping me to make corrections or to change the emphasis of a particular account.

Fred Gray also granted me four interviews, one at his office in Tuskegee, Alabama, and three by phone. None was as lengthy as the average interview with Claudette, but he generously answered all the questions I asked. Information from Alean Bowser, Annie Larkin Price, and Frank Sikora also derives from personal interviews.

The notes here refer to sources of quoted material. Unless otherwise noted, references are to books and articles cited in the bibliography.

PART ONE: FIRST CRY

1. JIM CROW AND THE NUMBER TEN

4   "The only professional jobs": Hampton and Fayer, *Voices of Freedom*, 18–19.

7   "The ten empty seats became": Robinson, *Montgomery Bus Boycott*, 35.

8   City ordinance since 1906: Garrow, "Origins," 22.

8   "There were no Negro drivers": King, *Stride Toward Freedom*, 40–41.

8   Stories about mistreatment of black bus riders: Robinson, *Montgomery Bus Boycott*, 7–9, 21–22; King, *Stride Toward Freedom*, 147–48.

2. COOT

15   Description of King Hill: Claudette's memories are supplemented by my own visit to the neighborhood on April 13, 2007. It had changed

very little from Claudette's girlhood. Neighbors were still close and knew one another well. The family who live in Claudette's old house invited me in to look around. They had heard her story and were proud to be living in the house in which Claudette Colvin had grown up.

19 St. Jude Hospital in Montgomery (sidebar): From the National Park Service's "We Shall Overcome: Historic Places of the Civil Rights Movement," http://www.nps.gov/history/nr/travel/civilrights/al5.htm.

3. "WE SEEMED TO HATE OURSELVES"

23 Tragedy struck once again: Jeremiah Reeves's arrest was not widely reported in local newspapers. The *Alabama Journal*, June 1, 1955, reports that the ongoing (second) trial was for "criminally assaulting a nineteen-year-old Cleveland Avenue housewife." An article in the *Montgomery Advertiser*, March 24, 1958, says Reeves was arrested in November 1952 for "raping a white woman."

23 "One of the authorities": King, *Stride Toward Freedom*, 31.

25 One Girl's Memory (sidebar): Author interview, March 27, 2007. The person quoted, a classmate of Claudette's, asked that she not be identified by name. The memory of Jeremiah Reeves never left this woman, or Claudette, or many other blacks who lived in Montgomery in those years. At 12:13 a.m. on March 28, 1958, Reeves was executed in the electric chair at Montgomery's Kilby State Prison. At the age of twenty-two, he had spent nearly six years on death row. Nine days after his death, on Easter Sunday, Martin Luther King, Jr., addressed two

thousand people on the steps of the Alabama State Capitol. "The issue before us now," he said, "is not the innocence or guilt of Jeremiah Reeves. Even if he were guilty, it is the severity and inequality of the penalty that constitutes the injustice. Full grown white men commiting comparable crimes against Negro girls are rarely if ever punished, and are never given the death penalty or even a life sentence . . . Easter is a day of hope . . . It is a day that says to us that the forces of evil and injustice cannot survive . . . We must live and face death if necessary with that hope." From *The Papers of Martin Luther King, Jr.,* vol. IV: *Symbol of a Movement, January 1957–December 1958.* "Statement Delivered at the Prayer Pilgrimage Protesting the Electrocution of Jeremiah Reeves," 6 April 1958. http://mlk-kpp01 .stanford.edu/primarydocuments/Vol4/6-Apr-1958_Jeremiah ReevesStatement.pdf.

Reeves's ordeal had a chilling effect on at least one black Montgomery boy. Fred Taylor was fourteen when Montgomery's buses were integrated. He later remembered, "I would sit [in the front of the bus] beside a white man, but I consciously did not sit by a white woman. I [could] remember a boy, Jeremiah Reeves, who got electrocuted for allegedly raping a white woman." Levine, *Freedom's Children,* 30.

29 "We conclude, unanimously" (*Brown v. Board* sidebar): Williams, *Eyes on the Prize,* 34–35.

5. "THERE'S THE GIRL WHO GOT ARRESTED"

39 "The wonderful thing": Younge, "She Would Not Be Moved."

39 "[With]in a few hours": Robinson, *Montgomery Bus Boycott*, 39.

40 "I felt like a dog": Robinson, *Montgomery Bus Boycott*, 15–17.

40 Robinson's victory with white merchants: Halberstam, *The Fifties*, 546.

42 "In Montgomery in 1955": Robinson, *Montgomery Bus Boycott*, 23.

44 "Both men were quite pleasant": King, *Stride Toward Freedom*, 41.

44 "hopeful": King, *Stride Toward Freedom*, 41.

44 "[We] were given to understand": Robinson, *Montgomery Bus Boycott*, 41.

46 Fred Gray's boyhood and law school education: Gray, *Bus Ride to Justice*, 3–15.

47 Fred Gray's visit to the Colvin family: Claudette's recollection; author interview with Fred Gray, Tuskegee, Alabama, April 11, 2007.

47 Citizens Coordinating Committee leaflet: Garrow, "Origins," 24.

48 Students remained in the hall: Author interview with Annie Larkin Price, Montgomery, Alabama, April 11, 2007. Ms. Price (then Annie Larkin) attended the March 18, 1955, hearing with several schoolmates.

48 "She insisted she was colored": Halberstam, *The Fifties*, 546.

49 "Claudette's agonized sobs": Robinson, *Montgomery Bus Boycott*, 42.

6. "CRAZY" TIMES

51 "The verdict was a bombshell": Robinson, *Montgomery Bus Boycott*, 42.

51 "The question of boycotting": Robinson, *Montgomery Bus Boycott*, 39.

52 Gossip about Claudette: Younge, "She Would Not Be Moved"; Willing, "Then Teens"; Branch, *Parting the Waters*, 123.

52 "I had to be sure": Williams, *Eyes on the Prize*, 63.

53 Church fund-raising for Claudette's lawsuit: King Papers, Stanford University, NAACP Notes.

53 "I just can't explain": King Papers, Stanford University, Letter from Virginia Durr to Curtis MacDougall.

54 May 6, 1955, appeal: Garrow, "Origins," 24; Branch, *Parting the Waters*, 123; Gray, *Bus Ride to Justice*, 49.

55 "From the time Claudette got arrested": Author interview with Alean Bowser, by telephone, March 27, 2007.

59 Mary Louise Smith's arrest: Willing, "Then Teens."

60 Gossip about Mary Louise Smith's family: Willing, "Then Teens"; Branch, *Parting the Waters*, 127.

60 "The inaction of the city": King, *Stride Toward Freedom*, 42.

7. "ANOTHER NEGRO WOMAN HAS BEEN ARRESTED"

63 "Another Negro woman has": Robinson, *Montgomery Bus Boycott*, 45.

69 "Just last Thursday": Branch, *Parting the Waters*, 139.

69 "And we are determined": Branch, *Parting the Waters*, 141.

70 MLK's Boyhood Bus Experience (sidebar): Garrow, *Bearing the Cross*, 35.

8. SECOND FRONT, SECOND CHANCE

73 "He had poetry in his voice": Williams and Greenhaw, *Thunder of Angels*, 85.

74 "Well, if you think" (sidebar): Garrow, *Bearing the Cross*, 22.

74 "I'd go home" (sidebar): Author interview with Annie Larkin Price, by telephone, February 19, 2007.

74 MIA network: Garrow, *Bearing the Cross*, 27.

76 "Jump in, grandmother": King, *Stride Toward Freedom*, 78.

76 "When they first sent the leaflets": Author interview with Alean Bowser, by telephone, March 27, 2007.

78 Juliette Morgan story (sidebar): Robinson, *Montgomery Bus Boycott*, 102–3.

79 "If I am stopped": King, *Stride Toward Freedom*, 138.

81 Fred Gray's strategy: Gray, *Bus Ride to Justice*, 68–70, and author interview with Fred Gray, Tuskegee, Alabama, April 11, 2007.

82 In 1900 . . . forty years later (sidebar): Newman and Sawyer, *Everybody Say Freedom*, 252.

82 Gray's plaintiff selection: Author interview with Fred Gray, Tuskegee, Alabama, April 11, 2007; telephone conversations, July 17 and August 20, 2007.

PART TWO: PLAYING FOR KEEPS

87 "All the boycotts": Sikora, *The Judge*, 229.

9. BROWDER V. GAYLE

90 "while they're juggling that hot potato": Johnson, "Bombing, Harassment Don't Stop," 11.

91 "That N—— who's running the bus boycott": Johnson, "Bombing, Harassment Don't Stop," 8.

92 "Are you looking for me?": Branch, *Parting the Waters*, 176.

93 "You could read a happiness": Williams and Greenhaw, *Thunder of Angels*, 212.

94 The description of the courtroom in which *Browder v. Gayle* was heard comes from two sources: Frank Sikora's *The Judge*, 17–18, and my own visit. I showed up at the federal courthouse in Montgomery, now named after Judge Johnson, on April 10, 2007. Two uniformed guards informed me that I would not be able to visit the courtroom unless I had official business, but one guard agreed to telephone a clerk who worked for Judge Edward Carnes, now in charge of Judge Johnson's courtroom, to see if he would allow me to visit. To everyone's surprise, he agreed. Soon the clerk and I were standing in a beautifully paneled courtroom, bathed in sunlight pouring in from high, vaulted windows. I gazed up at a ceiling inlaid with bright Spanish tiles. It was a Southern courthouse reminiscent of the one in *To Kill a Mockingbird*, and in mint condition. I was permitted to make sketches of the room but not to take photos. The clerk kindly answered my many questions about the typical movements of plaintiffs, defendants, judges, audience members, and other court officials.

94 The description of the hearing, *Browder v. Gayle*, comes almost entirely from Frank Sikora's book *The Judge*, about the life and principal cases of Judge Frank M. Johnson. As the sidebar on page 93 shows, Judge Johnson's decisions during the civil rights years had a huge impact on the South. The first major case presented in *The Judge* is *Browder v. Gayle*. Sikora interviewed Judge Johnson at length about the case, including the judge's memories and impressions of Claudette Colvin's testimony. When I write, for example, that Claudette "widened" her eyes in talking to City Attorney Knabe, that memory or impression comes from Judge Johnson, as told to Frank Sikora (who was not in the courtroom that day). Sikora also unearthed the transcript of the hearing—the court clerk's written record of exactly what everyone said—to help prompt Judge Johnson's memory of events that had taken place several decades before their conversation. All who realize the great importance of *Browder v. Gayle*—the first major federal court verdict to go beyond schools in ruling that racial segregation in public facilities was unconstitutional—owe a debt of gratitude to Frank Sikora.

10. RAGE IN MONTGOMERY

103 "Judge, as far as I'm concerned": Sikora, *The Judge*, 35–37.

104 "If I had been in your shoes": Sikora, *The Judge*, 41.

104 "We hold that the statutes" (sidebar): Sikora, *The Judge*, 38–39.

107 "My heart began to throb": King, *Stride Toward Freedom*, 160.

107 "I rode the bus" (sidebar): Author interview with Annie Larkin Price, by telephone, February 19, 2007.

107 "Darling," she explained, "the bus boycott" (sidebar): Levine, *Freedom's Children*, 31.

108 "we will continue to walk": Branch, *Parting the Waters*, 194.

108 "I guess we'll have to abide": Sikora, *The Judge*, 43.

109 "I was cooking": Hampton and Fayer, *Voices of Freedom*, 32.

109 "I believe you are": King, *Stride Toward Freedom*, 173.

109 "It is interesting": Sikora, *The Judge*, 44.

110 "We had gotten there": Author interview with Annie Larkin Price, Montgomery, Alabama, April 13, 2007.

110 "The issue now has passed": *Montgomery Advertiser*, editorial, January 14, 1956.

EPILOGUE

115 "I was met at the door": Author interview with Frank Sikora, by telephone, August 2007.

ACKNOWLEDGMENTS

I thank Dianne and Clyde Jones for allowing me to walk through Claudette's childhood home in King Hill when I visited Montgomery for research. Jeanne Smiley, the niece of Geraldine Nesbitt, kindly drove me around the city, pointing out landmarks of the bus protest and of her youth. I'm deeply grateful to Alean Bowser and Annie Larkin Price for talking with me and providing photographs. I thank the famed civil rights attorney Fred Gray, who answered my questions at his law offices in Tuskegee and afterward by phone.

For advice, wisdom, connections, and overall resourcefulness, I thank Georgette Norman, director of the Rosa Parks Library and Museum. Norwood Kerr and Meredith McLemore of the Alabama State Archives provided helpful research assistance, as did Linda Harvey of Alabama State University.

For help in obtaining photographs and rights to publish them, I thank Kenneth Hare, Wanda Lloyd, and Karen Doerr of the *Montgomery Advertiser*; John Thorp of the Jim Crow Museum at Ferris State University; Claudette's sister Gloria Laster; Ashni Mohnot of the Martin Luther King,

Jr., Research and Education Institute; Penny Weaver; Laura Anderson of the Birmingham Civil Rights Museum; Judge Reese McKinney, Jr.; Tricia O'Connor of the Children's Museum of Indianapolis; and John Broderick.

This book would not exist without the generosity of the *USA Today* reporter Richard Willing, who put me in touch with Claudette. I thank my longtime friend and editor Melanie Kroupa for her faith in this book and skill in helping me create it. Once again, Melanie's assistant, Sharon McBride, helped immensely. Thanks to Grace Hine for all she taught me. I thank Kirsten Cappy of Curious City for insightfully commenting on an early draft of the book. Thanks to Cheryl Hart, Toby Hollander, and Ruby and Hannah Hoose for reading portions of the manuscript as it was in production, and for letting me read to them. Sandra Lee Ste. George shared this book's creation intimately with me from first page to last.

Most of all, I thank Claudette Colvin for taking a chance on a writer she had never heard of. I hope I earned her trust.

PICTURE CREDITS

Every effort has been made to trace the copyright holders, and we apologize for any unintentional omissions. We would be pleased to insert the appropriate acknowledgment in any subsequent edition of this book.

INDEX

ABOUT THE AUTHOR

PHILLIP HOOSE's distinguished nonfiction books for garnered many honors, including a Newbery Hond Award, the *Boston Globe–Horn Book* Award for Nonfict the Christopher Award, and the Flora Stieglitz Straus

It was while writing the 2001 National Book Awa *There, Too! Young People in U.S. History* that the a Claudette Colvin. Intrigued, he became intent on lear discovered was the all-but-overlooked story of a smart made two major contributions to the civil rights move

Mr. Hoose lives in Maine with his wife, Sandi Ste. formation about Mr. Hoose and his work, visit www.p